A History of Yorktown and its Victory Celebrations

A HISTORY OF YORKTOWN AND ITS VICTORY CELEBRATIONS

Revival to Patriotism

KATHLEEN MANLEY

THE
History
PRESS

Published by The History Press
Charleston, SC 29403
www.historypress.net

Cover image: Marching in the military review, October 19, 1931, military volunteers are costumed as Washington's continentals. *Courtesy of the O'Hara Collection.*

First published 2005

ISBN 978.1.59629.078.5

Library of Congress Cataloging-in-Publication Data

Manley, Kathleen.
Revival to patriotism : a history of Yorktown, Virginia and its victory
celebrations / Kathleen Manley.
p. cm.
Includes bibliographical references.
ISBN 978-1-59629-078-5 (alk. paper)
1. Yorktown (Va.)--History. 2. Yorktown (Va.)--Anniversaries, etc. 3.
Yorktown (Va.)--Social life and customs. 4.
Patriotism--Virginia--Yorktown--History. 5. Political
culture--Virginia--Yorktown--History. 6.
Festivals--Virginia--Yorktown--History. 7.
Monuments--Virginia--Yorktown--History. I. Title.
F234.Y6M35 2005
975.5'423--dc22
2005022184

Even as much as the country needs a business revival, it likewise needs a revival of patriotism.

Franklin D. Roosevelt
1931 Sesquicentennial Celebration

CONTENTS

ACKNOWLEDGEMENTS

The source of my devotion and interest in the subject of Yorktown began with the study of my mother's personal collection of books, newspaper clippings, pictures, literature and family genealogy. To my dearest mother, my first English teacher, Doris Lincoln Manley, I dedicate this book.

It was of considerable help to have made the acquaintance of James Haskett, retired historian for the National Park Service at Yorktown. I thank him tremendously for his help with the elusive subject matter of some of these celebrations. The information about the organizational aspects of some of these large celebrations goes largely unreported. It is for his carefully kept records and attention to details that I express my gratitude.

My special thanks to Claudia Jew at the Mariners Museum and Dale Neighbors at the Library of Virginia for the important images that they made possible.

It is also noteworthy that Melonie Fedorchak was such a tremendous help with the scanning of some of the images.

Because I grew up in Yorktown, I have come to know many of the local people. My thanks to my childhood neighbor Margaret Cook, with the Swem Library, for her effort to give me important information in the last days before my deadline.

Debby Padgett provided helpful guidance for the 1957 chapter on Jamestown—her suggestions made for a more informational chapter.

Special thanks for the cooperation of Bonnie and Jerry Karwac Jr. in donating the images from their private collection. These images give the reader a tangible view of souvenirs and items that were available in the 1881 and 1931 celebrations. I give my grateful thanks.

To the good people, Mr. and Mrs. James O'Hara for their contribution. My thanks can never be enough for their interest and support of my projects.

Importantly, I want to thank and praise the talented and award-winning artist Hazel Burt Camp for the original sketch in this book. Also, my most appreciative thanks for the original art donated by artist John Hall.

Lastly, and certainly not least, my grateful thanks to The History Press that made this book possible, specifically Jason Chasteen, Julie Hiester, Kirsten Sutton, Amanda Lidderdale and all those that worked on the various aspects of this book. I think I speak for all regional authors in thanking this publisher and all others who take an interest in local and regional important data.

CONTRIBUTIONS
THAT CHANGED YORKTOWN

G reat sacrifice, many contributions and the cooperation of civic and governmental organizations have changed the structure and size of Yorktown. The scope and size of each celebration is by no means best understood in any publication. Only the attendance of these intriguing collaborations can give the observer feelings that will remain for a lifetime of memories. With uniqueness unto itself, each celebration can be seen with circumstances and events that are reflective of the times and the politics in America. For those who visit or live within this history, it is a path of wisdom unlike any other experience.

Every year brings a special commemoration on October 19, Yorktown Day. The historical facts of these previous celebrations have been consolidated but recorded for the important history of Yorktown. Along with the details of the major events of 1824, 1881, 1931, 1957 and 1981, larger than usual events are noteworthy on several dates.

Special plans were created for Yorktown Day, October 19, 1837, and written about in the *Southern Literary Messenger.* In the edition dated December 1837, details of the ceremonies included an address by the Honorable John Tyler. The sponsor that year was the "Williamsburg Guards." Later, as the preliminary event of 1881, the celebration of 1879 was a colorful event recorded in *Frank Leslie's Illustrated Newspaper*, New York, November 8, 1879. The article details "vessels of the North Atlantic Squadron rode at anchor off the town [and were] handsomely decked out with national colors." At the close of the program the military and invited guests were entertained with a huge barbeque on the lawn in front of the Nelson House. After the large event of 1881 there were the celebrations of the 1900s. Some events, which were organized around 1909, were sponsored by the Yorktown Historical Society. Following tradition, various historical groups of the village and the peninsula sponsored the anniversary ceremonies. With the establishment of the Comte de Grasse Chapter of the Daughters of the American Revolution in Yorktown in 1922, Yorktown Day was more continuously celebrated. By 1932, events were jointly sponsored by the Daughters of the American Revolution, the Yorktown Day Association, various patriotic organizations and the Colonial National Historical Park.

The Yorktown Day Association was formed in August of 1949 with their activities being that of planning patriotic exercises on Yorktown Day each year. The Daughters of the American Revolution celebrated their twenty-fifth ceremony of sponsorship that same year and there was inspiration among other groups to form a committee. Thirteen groups now form the association and work together to plan activities each year to commemorate the victory at Yorktown of the American Revolutionary War.

Since the town's beginnings, roads have been rerouted and new buildings have come into existence. Few people realize were it not for the Sesquicentennial preparations in 1930, no one could cruise down the hill beside the monument on Comte Grasse Street, or pass by the new court house on Ballard Street. Surrender Road was added for the celebration grounds. The construction of all these streets was created to accommodate the traffic congestion of 1931.

Buildings such as the Victory Center, created by the Jamestown-Yorktown Foundation and the construction and rebuilding of the visitors' centers at Yorktown and Jamestown have continued the ongoing achievement of educating the world to the history of Yorktown.

With the decline of the tobacco trade after the late eighteenth century, Yorktown began to retreat to the quaint acceptability of a comfortable hometown, only noteworthy to the citizens that grew up there. But Yorktown was historically famous and so in a quiet prideful desperation, the people of Yorktown invited the powerful unity of the United States congressional influence and local politics to preserve their history. In an effort to give the town to the world, Yorktown had to become a national monument. Yorktown was first destroyed by war and then by fire, and the storm of 1933 but undaunted the tiny town rebuilt.

In times of peace and war, the people of Yorktown took proud ownership in their hometown. The pride and unabashed love of the history of America and Yorktown, with all of the local historical organizations, continues to be a strong source of goodwill and work in the town. It is obvious that the culmination of sacrifice with blood and passion during the American Revolutionary War brought victory in Yorktown in 1781, and in so doing, brought cause for celebration.

With the 1824 tour of General Lafayette, a passionate, wealthy advocate for democracy, a tradition had begun that has been faithfully observed, with the exception of that year, every fifty years since the time of the surrender in Yorktown on October 19, 1781. Forty-three years after the surrender of Britian, the most beloved General Lafayette toured America, visiting Yorktown on one of his stops. Invited expressly because his leadership was important in the success of the final campaign in Yorktown, Lafayette and the local townspeople wanted to celebrate once again in the place that had made the general so famous.

The town returned to its quaintness while waiting and watching for the next fifty-seven years to commemorate the Victory Monument that was promised to them at the end of the Revolutionary War. The time had finally come. Armed with appropriations from Congress, the Victory Monument could finally be built. Tens of thousands of people turned out for a preliminary celebration that proved a success two years before to what became known as the 1881 Centennial of Yorktown. With Masons in force to oversee the laying of the cornerstone, along with fifty thousand visitors, the town was host to a larger celebration than expected. Then, in what seemed like no time at all, America was in the shadows of the Great Depression and looking at another celebratory Sesquicentennial year of the surrender at Yorktown in 1931.

The 1920s had come in with a roar, thereby creating great wealth and poverty as America became an industrial nation. By 1931, the American economy was rebuilding, as was Yorktown. During the years that led up to the celebration, important men and women breathed life into the beginnings of Yorktown as a national monument. Yorktown was without electricity, telephone and telegraph services, water or improved roadways. The celebration that taught future organizers how to plan brought all these things to the town. But Yorktown was not alone—the historical triangle was organizing and Jamestown was also having important celebrations since its 1607 beginnings.

In 1957, Yorktown saw many important changes as a result of the tourism of Jamestown's 350th Anniversary. Projects that had begun with the establishment of Colonial National Park Service were in need of modern renovations. Much was done and redone to accommodate a large celebration that would include Queen Elizabeth, her husband Prince Phillip and the Queen Mother of England. But when larger tourism numbers were becoming a factor that seemed most formidable, the years of 1976 and 1981 loomed in the future.

The White House issued a decree that all national parks would be fully operational with new innovations and exhibits for the nation's celebration in 1976. The National Park Service entered into a pace of renovation that was thought to be impossible. When all tasks were accomplished, the 1981 celebration preparations began. The surrender at Yorktown was two hundred years past and the largest festival in the history of Yorktown became a reality on October 16–19, 1981. With the nation traveling easily through modern aviation, rail systems and the automobile, Yorktown was going to see tourism at the highest numbers ever. Festival tents were set with entertainment from across the nation. Revolutionary War reenactors came by the thousands to camp on the battlefields. Every organization dedicated to preservation donned their costumes and participated. Yorktown got another sprucing up to meet the challenge of hosting America's independence birthday party.

The facts of each celebration are fascinating and in some cases staggering to conceive. But when all was finished, troops departed and the last of the tent poles were taken down for transportation out of town, Yorktown was rewarded for having acquisitions, new buildings and more notoriety than ever before. A revival to patriotism is an ongoing business that never seems to stop fascinating and captivating the world. It will continue with the festivals and celebrations of the year 2006, and the newest contribution, the revitalization of the York River waterfront addition—Riverwalk Landing.

It is important to note that no record or official recollection of the 1981 celebration was ever written. Well-researched publications by the federal and state government produced recollections of the celebrations of 1881, 1931 and 1957. This recording is by no means meant to recall or detail every event of these enormous undertakings. But for the sake of history, this small version of the events at least tells most of the superficial aspects of the glorious days that will forever remain among Yorktown's proudest moments.

THE RETURN OF LAFAYETTE IN 1824

G eneral Lafayette returned to Yorktown, in October of 1824, and so began a history of ceremony and festivals that still invites crowds of patriotic people from all over the world. The festivities of 1824 were plagued with time constraints, lack of funds and workmen to build a proper celebration area, yet still, the descriptions of the ceremony are remarkable and stand as a beginning to celebrations of 1881, 1931, 1957 and 1981.

At the request of President James Monroe, General Lafayette arrived with his son, George Washington Lafayette; his secretary, Auguste Levasseur; and a valet, Bastien, on August 15, 1824, only to delay his arrival overnight in New York City, due to Sunday Sabbath laws. Following the month-long journey to America aboard the *Cadmus* at the age of sixty-seven, the revered hero of the American Revolutionary War was invited back and supplied with every comfort both in travel and lodging. Never a penny of his own money was to be spent for his visit to America because Lafayette was "a guest of the nation." Everywhere that the general went he drew enormous crowds. Disembarking at the battery of New York City to tens of thousands of cheering people, led to a procession up Broadway lined with another fifty thousand people, then to City Hall where the mayor welcomed him. A most beloved man of the democratic freedom had come to visit all the people of America and lavish preparations were laid before him everywhere that he was received. More than one author has thrilled at the historical opportunity of detailing how the "nation's guest" sat between Thomas Jefferson and James Madison at a banquet planned during the visit to Charlottesville.

In 1777, as a man of twenty years old and the youngest major general in the American Army at the Battle of Brandywine, Lafayette was introduced to his fellow officers, Captain John Marshall, twenty-two; Colonel James Monroe, nineteen; Colonel Alexander Hamilton, nineteen; and Captain Aaron Burr, twenty-one. Having joined George Washington's staff, a close friendship grew between Washington and Lafayette. Lafayette in later years named his son after Washington and, later, visited Mount Vernon on many occasions. It was Lafayette's steadfast intense desire to pursue liberty at all costs—including spending a large portion of his own fortune in this single endeavor.

With the passing of forty-seven years since Lafayette and James Monroe had served together in the Army, now Monroe, as president of the United States, would be taken with a sentimental request from his ambassador to France, Albert Gallatin, a close friend. Gallatin knew that Lafayette wanted to return to the United States and asked Monroe to extend an invitation, after a resolution in Congress, to bring back the war hero to visit his friends and comrades in arms, and give America yet another slice of "the era of good feelings."

President James Monroe, a lifelong Virginian, resembled George Washington— tall for a man of his time with lean prominent bones of the face and body, and a strong military reputation. These qualities were not unlike Lafayette's. In 1816, at the time of his presidential inauguration, Monroe was wearing his hair old fashioned in a powdered queue tied at the back. He wore suits of black broadcloth with knee breeches and buckles on his shoes, which were the fashion in the years when America won its freedom in 1781.

Monroe was minister to France in 1794 during Washington's term as president, and then later during the Jefferson administration he helped negotiate the purchase of New Orleans. It only seems all the more evident that such a generous invitation to Lafayette would come during his own presidential administration.

The First Celebration

With the passing of forty-three years after the surrender, the celebration would begin with Lafayette's return on October 18, 1824. Lafayette landed and made his way through some of the Northern cities including his stop at Washington, D.C. According to the *Norfolk and Portsmouth Herald*, the smoke of the distant steamships could be seen on the eastern horizon and indicated the procession of ships. Lafayette changed steamboats at Old Point Comfort to the *Virginia*, which had a cannon on the bow and fired in salute as the general arrived. The steamboats, crowded with passengers, had arrived early that morning to Yorktown prior to the general. Then, as the illustrious guest arrived, there was much saluting with military music and cannon fire between the steamships, which was an exciting arrival for all who waited on the shore. That newspaper also wrote:

> *The moment was a precious one to those who then, for the first beheld, the man for who they had cherished such exalted sentiments of gratitude, admiration and affection; every eye was fixed in a steady gaze upon his venerable figure as he ascended the side of the vessel and scarcely moved but to follow him as he passed along the deck.*

At half past one, the steamship *Virginia* dropped anchor and awaited the arrival of the *Petersburg* carrying Lafayette. Filled with exhilaration and anxiety, the crowed watched a pontoon that was launched, as the water levels would not accommodate a large ship all the way to shore. The place for arrival was assured by flagstaff. In admiration and protection the Richmond and Portsmouth Volunteer Artillery skillfully watched from one hundred feet above the beach.

Arches

Two hundred yards to the right of the landing and elevated on the bluff was the redoubt where Lafayette had stormed the British troops on October 17, 1781. It was there that a triumphal arch stood. The arch, showing only on the field side, was situated so close to the bluff that it could not be approached by the river. Apparently time and lack of workmen and artists compelled the committee to decide this design. The arch was forty-five feet in height with a large eagle adorning the top, looking much like that of a chapel in Rome. The wooden arch was decorated to imitate sculptured marble; the front was painted a light brownish stone color. Thirteen key stones resembling white marble shown with a star in relief on each, corresponded to the thirteen original states of the Union. The bottom of the columns had emblems and symbols of unity and implements of war. The entablature was supported by four columns of pilasters. Between the two pilasters on each side were figures—one representing justice and liberty trampling upon tyranny. Over the arch were two names, "Hamilton" and "Laurens," along with the name Lafayette, in large letters immediately under the eagle.

The stage was set. With the *Petersburg* securely anchored, the crowds above on the bluffs waited for their hero to come ashore. For a quarter of a mile, the bluff was lined with groups of spectators. In the river below, for nearly the same distance, numerous small vessels, nearly a hundred sails, waited with decks crowded with admiring spectators. The governor stood with the Executive Council of Virginia

Victory arch. *Courtesy of John Hall.*

and the General Committee of Arrangements to greet many lofty and well-known military figures of war hero status, along with the president of the court of appeals, the chief justice of the United States, John Marshall, Colonel Fish and Colonel McLane (the only surviving members from the last battle of Yorktown), among others, at the landing. Last, but certainly not least, "a company of ladies, among [whom] were some of Virginia's fairest daughters," were greeted as well. Awaiting the arrival was a superb barouche from Richmond, and carriages for the other distinguished civil and military people, along with a long procession of citizens on horseback and on foot, which were organized and in fine order.

On October 18, 1824, at two o'clock, the "Guest of the Nation" landed in Yorktown in the midst of a thunder of artillery from several of the vessels on the river and from the cliffs above. Thousands of cheering spectators blended with military music that gave great acclamation on the bluffs and the beaches below. As Lafayette stepped upon Virginian soil, the governor received him with a heartfelt welcoming speech, which Lafayette returned remarks in brief.

But for the preparations made for the general's arrival, Yorktown had not been rebuilt and was still in ruins. Blackened by fire or pierced by bullets, the ground was covered with fragments of weapons, broken shells and overturned gun carriages. "On every part of the battle ground were to be found balls, shells and fragment of bombs, the interesting evidences of the ardour and peril with which the capture of York was characterized." Some later information sources raised the question that perhaps the scene was contrived for the town to look as it had during the Revolutionary War.

Obelisks

A seventy-six foot obelisk was constructed in range of the arch at a distance of two hundred yards. Aside from the base decorations of battle-axes, these pedestals were erected to designate the British redoubt stormed by the French troops. There were ornaments descriptive of fame, valor, prudence and victory engraved on the obelisk.

Four hundred yards farther within that line of encampment, a second obelisk was erected on the spot where the sword of the British general was surrendered. Written on the sides of the obelisk were the words "Washington, First in War, First in Peace," and on the other side, "First in the hearts of his countrymen." The column was decorated with emblems of General George Washington, war, peace and agriculture, as well as the names of the military generals in battle. The column was painted to look like stone and designed by Mr. Swaine, an architect in Richmond.

Lafayette was then pointed to his barouche, accompanied by the governor and the chief justice, and then other carriages filled with the whole procession, which moved through a double row of spectators that filed in behind, all the way

Lafayette's arrival on Main Street. *Courtesy of John Hall.*

cheering and shouting enthusiastic joy. The carriages carried their parties to the house of Thomas Nelson, Esquire, who politely gave his home to the committee for Lafayette's visit. At Nelson's mansion, a double row of militia officers, acting as a guard of honor, were arranged on each side of the walk from the court gate to the door.

After rising from a half an hour rest Lafayette was overwhelmed when he tried to leave the Nelson House with a throng of spectators in the front of the house. It was so immense that upon his exit, Lafayette was caught by an enthusiastic crowd reaching for his hand, first one and then another with such force that the general was led back to the house. With the general retiring, the marshals set up a passage opening only wide enough for one person to pass at a time along by the gate. The general then reappeared at the gate and affectionately met each member of the audience as they extended their hand.

On the beautiful front lawn of the Nelson House, "forming a summit of a lofty eminence," a spacious tent of nearly one hundred feet was pitched, with a large dome in the center from which waved a star-spangled banner, and a wing of the tent that extended to about fifty feet. This served as a dining place for the general and other distinguished people. Under the wings were two rows of tables, and under the dome a circular table allowed a continuation of the passage between the guests seated under the wing. The tent of General George Washington was brought down from Fort McHenry, carried ashore and pitched by a group of committee volunteers who placed it behind the grand dining tent.

Within the town, approximately a mile down Hampton Road (now Cooke Road), quarters for the generals and administration of the various participating artilleries were encamped. The town had been converted into a camp with the harbor filled with steamboats and other vessels. Among the commanders present were such men as Generals Cocke and Brodnax, Colonel Nimmo and, under his command, Lieutenant Colonel Abraham Eustis. Having prepared these encampments in the previous week, the officers had a role in setting and keeping order for the event. Eleven companies of United States troops and fifteen to twenty companies of Virginia volunteers paraded on the battlefield. The estimated crowds numbered ten to fifteen thousand people. The celebration being successfully carried out, it became a small blueprint for future celebrations.

On the morning of October 19, the troops stood in review for the "venerable hero" and formed a line on the riverbank, extending from the left side of the arch, where the redoubt had once been, and the volunteer artillery to the right. Established the day before, the committee had set up a processional line starting at the Nelson House and extending down Main Street in the direction of the Hampton Highway. Turning left, the processional line extended to the arch on the battlefield. With all the best intentions, the throngs of spectators completely blocked the avenue. It took the marshals some time to clear the path for Lafayette to proceed. General Lafayette and the troops marched up and took their places at the arch for a review of the military battalions. Having given his approval, Lafayette made his way down the line, boarded his barouche and rode on with all other carriages behind. With the military units leading, the parade continued down Hampton Highway to a stage that had been erected (two hundred feet in length with rows of seats "ascending one above another") for the use of the ladies that had come for the parade. The seats were completely filled with, as the *Norfolk and Portsmouth Herald* newspaper described it, a "more captivating display of female loveliness we will venture to say has seldom been witnessed in this or any other country." With Lafayette being a widower for several years, the ladies gathered everywhere he went on his tour. In this case, the paper reported the ladies did not "exceed a thousand." As the columns of military passed a stage for review, along with the general, every lady was waving a handkerchief or a parasol. Lafayette, with an uncovered head, passed slowly, bowing his head gracefully as he passed. The *Herald* described the scene: "Rising above the tops of their heads, [could be] seen the tops of the arch, and obelisk near it [with] no background but the blue vault of the heavens, serene and cloudless."

Later that afternoon at the Nelson House, dinner was served for the general and high dignitaries and volunteers under the great tent on the lawn. There Lafayette was heard to say, "Patriots who fought without pay, without clothing and without murmuring," and, "York Town: and may the pretensions and the arms of the usurpers of National Rights, every where be surrendered to popular good sense, and patriotic energy." A rousing tribute to General Lafayette was also made: "The laurel wreath around his brow, is the evergreen of fame, which wintry time shall not wither, but mature." Lafayette spoke in memory of Col. Scammell and the Soldiers of both nations, French and American who fell at Yorktown, "Our Country—What envious foe can deny that she is lovely? Let every American revere her as his mother, and love her as the bride of his heart."

That same evening, the general proceeded to the encampment as he had the evening before, and looked on a "brilliant exhibition of fire works" that concluded the day's ceremonies. Upon his return to the Nelson House, volunteers had unearthed an old trunk thought to be from the days of the Revolution, along with some candles blackened with age. In ceremony to the victory, the candles were lit in a circle in the center of the lawn to define an area where dancing took place that evening. In a diary of events during the tour in Yorktown, Auguste Levasseur, Lafayette's secretary, wrote,

A ball in Yorktown in 1824 by the light of Cornwallis candles appeared so pleasant to the old revolutionary soldiers, that not withstanding their great age,

A dance with Lafayette. *Courtesy of the Hazel Burt Camp Collection.*

voluntary soldiers, and the fatigues of the day, most were unwilling to retire until the candles were entirely consumed.

At dawn the troops departed and a military breakfast was held on the battlefield for the guests. By two in the afternoon, Lafayette was gone to Williamsburg.

In the days that followed, Lafayette toured Williamsburg, and Levasseur reported that the town was "a small town…at present retaining very little of its ancient importance." Bemoaning the decidedly decayed state of the College of William and Mary and after attending a banquet and a ball in his honor, Lafayette's travels took him to Jamestown where he boarded the *Petersburg* for Norfolk. Few details exist of Norfolk, as Levasseur apparently did not care for the city, saying "Of all the cities we visited Norfolk had the least agreeable aspect. The houses are generally badly built and the streets narrow and crooked. On account of the adjacent marshes the air is unhealthy and diseases common during the autumn." With only a short time in Norfolk, the party departed to Richmond.

In Richmond, Fredericksburg and other towns in the South, slaves and freed

Negroes were prohibited from the ceremonies of Lafayette's visit. Yet, Lafayette received blacks and Indians with great enthusiasm, remembering them in great detail when they had personal conversations. Although Lafayette did not proclaim his antislavery views during this visit, a Negro pushed past some armed sentinels posted at the door in Columbia, South Carolina, and proclaimed that he had come to see the general. Lafayette turned, looked at him and remarked, "An old acquaintance; don't tell me who it is." As the Negro approached the general, bowing his head he held out his hand and said, "Howdy, Mas'Lafayette; how do you do sir. You 'member me?"

"Yes, stop; don't tell me your name. Ah! I have it. Pompey, belonging to General Buchanan." Lafayette then asked for a glass of champagne with Pompey and the two toasted together their acquaintance in years gone by. Pompey put out his hand and said, "Good-bye, Mas'Lafayette; we are getting old—we'll never meet again. God bless you." They shook hands and Pompey left, mounting his pony for his journey home.

Lafayette brought a patriotic fervor and renewed interest in the country since the surrender of the British; his impression on Yorktown was indelibly marked. The settlement of so many political issues loomed large in the United States, with many days ahead of great joy and sadness. Lafayette lived only another ten years after he left the United States. While attending a funeral, the general contracted pneumonia and never recovered.

THE CENTENNIAL
OF 1881

In the heat of July 2, 1881, unaccompanied by secret service (as was the practice of the time), President James Garfield may have been miles away in his mind from the business of Washington that day. The news sources talked of corruption, fraud, spoils and all the pressure of the election the previous year. But for the moment, Garfield looked forward to going to his twenty-fifth college reunion. Standing on the train station platform, he no doubt contemplated his success, and his classmates surely looked forward to seeing their friend, the president of the United States. Without any warning, Garfield was shot twice. As soon as the shots were fired, Charles J. Guiteau, a political opponent disgruntled in not receiving the United States consul to Paris cried, "I am a Stalwart and Arthur is President now!"

Yorktown Victory Monument

The assassin was arrested immediately, tried and hung the next year. Garfield lived for eighty days after the shooting. Doctors knew he still suffered from one of his wounds but without X-rays they could not find the bullet. A wounded Garfield lay dying, unable to recover. On September 18, 1881, President Garfield died and Chester Arthur was later sworn in the oath of office. In October 1881, as one of his first official duties, Arthur arrived in Yorktown along with tens of thousands of Masons to officiate the laying of the cornerstone to the long-awaited Victory Monument.

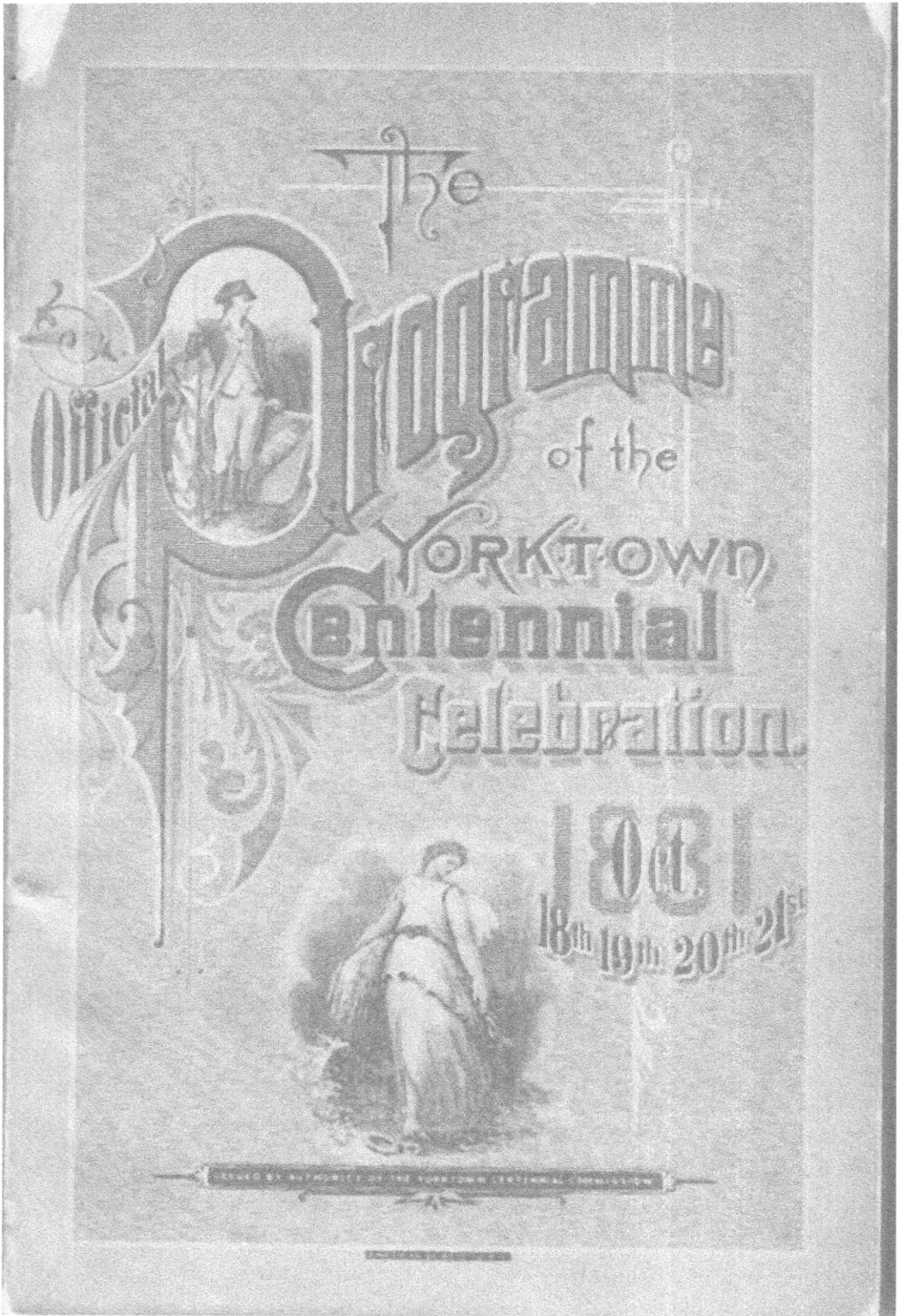

Cover of the Centennial program of events. *Courtesy of the Karwac Collection.*

Years before, in 1878, in Norfolk, a Virginian, Michael Glennan, a poor immigrant boy from Ireland, began to correspond with Hugh Blair Grigsby, president of the Virginia Historical Society and chancellor of the College of William and Mary. Glennan, editor and sole proprietor of the *Norfolk Virginian*, having known of the Centennial Celebration of Bunker Hill, began to promote a similar idea and to have Yorktown properly celebrated with their own centennial of the victory in Yorktown.

The Continental Congress had approved a monument at Yorktown on October 29, 1781, but funds were not appropriated until one hundred years later. In 1879, governors of the thirteen original states met at Independence Hall in Philadelphia, Pennsylvania, and with appropriations finally in place, the commemoration plans could begin with Michael Glennan playing a prominent part in the celebration.

On Thursday, October 23, 1879, a smaller event took place to test the level of likely community participation. Thankfully, ten thousand people from various states participated with military and naval displays that were very impressive. With the assurance of the attendance that year, national and local planning committees could begin to form.

In the following year, prior to the official start of the Centennial, the mayor of Norfolk proclaimed a special week of festivities beginning October 15, and invited the British vessels docked at the wharves to participate in a seaside festival. The official national ceremonies began on October 18 and ran through October 20, 1881, but there were various events in Yorktown starting on the thirteenth, and some that continued in Richmond until the twenty-sixth.

With great excitement, more celebrities attended Yorktown's 1881 Centennial than the opening of the 1876 World's Fair in Philadelphia. Fifty thousand people jammed the streets of the town with the eager intention of knowing an important historical place. There were members of the Cabinet, Congress and the Supreme Court as well as military forces, all with their officers of important rank. Also attending was the portly General Fitzhugh Lee, commander of the Brigade of Virginia Volunteers, who would be governor of the state in later years. Orders of many Masonic Lodges were in attendance contrasting with political elite: former Presidents Ulysses Grant and Rutherford Hayes, former Vice Presidents Hannibal Hamlin, Schuyler Colfax and William A. Wheeler.

America had awaited a monument for nearly one hundred years as Congress resolved in 1781 that a "marble column, adorned with emblems of the alliance between the U.S. and his Most Christian Majesty," would be constructed. With so much politics and so little time or money, the issue of basic authority was raised again in 1875 by historian George Bancroft, who wrote to the mayor of Newport, Rhode Island, in June pointing out that Congress had indeed pledged

"Arriving Troops." *Courtesy of the Library of Virginia.*

Lapel Ribbon, 1881. *Karwac Collection.*

to build this monument. This letter and various memorials were a part of the initial movement that finally began the work of the Hallowell, Maine, granite shaft that stands today.

Plans for the Festivities

To prepare for the great event, Yorktown was converted to a mass tent city. In the first of this kind of celebration the troops camped in and around the Moore House, where the surrender had been negotiated in 1781. Masonic orders and armies erected temporary housing of twelve hundred army hospital tents.

Still visible were the trenches, gun emplacements and breastworks from the Civil War. The historic atmosphere of walking in the soldiers' paths, no doubt, gave pause to all in attendance.

Guests arriving by river were able to use temporary wharves at the end of Ballard Street, with commercial vessels as well as Navy ships disembarking thousands of spectators in Yorktown. To spectators walking up the hill to Main Street, Yorktown was a treat—looking quaint and old English, yet shabby from years of neglect. Standing tall through the years of neglect were the houses that had survived in 1781, along with newer hotels, restaurants, makeshift theaters and eating places.

French guests began to arrive in New York on October 5 and were given a reception along with a military review. Baltimore, Richmond and Norfolk also staged events and parties. A parade and review on October 10, 1881, marked

Surrender scene medallion, 1881. *Courtesy of the Karwac Collection.*

preliminary celebrations. Unlike Yorktown, that was without electric lights, the city of Baltimore staged a grand illumination using electric and calcium lights, to begin the celebration. Along with this gala parade, athletic events were scheduled on the second day, as well as concerts and Naval parades in the harbor. Fireworks finished the activities on the night of October 12, 1881.

In Washington, French and German guests were feted with a formal reception on October 13. The next day military and civic escorts paraded the distinguished guests to the Capitol for a reception in the rotunda. There were more fireworks that night in Washington, followed by an excursion to Mount Vernon. Two days later, there was a reception at the home of Secretary of State James Gillespie Blaine. October 16, following church services, guests departed by boat to Yorktown at 6:00 p.m.

The Coming of the C&O

The only transportation to and from the peninsula was by water. The enthusiasm and excitement was building as the local population dreamed of overland connections to the great wide north and western parts of the country. In 1871, Collis P. Huntington directed that surveys be carried out for an extension of the railroad. The plans were to go eastward from Richmond, to one of five deep-water harbors. The harbors were the mouth of the Piankatank River or Newport News, West Point, Norfolk and Yorktown.

Greedy landowners clashed with politicians who wanted the transportation growth. Yorktown was seriously considered as a final destination city over Newport News because of the shorter track mileage to Richmond. Yorktown's notoriety had also been growing as the Centennial celebration approached. But when Huntington's intentions to purchase became local news, the price of real estate skyrocketed. Disgusted, Huntington turned his eyes to Newport News.

Still Yorktown's prominence in the upcoming celebration could not be ignored. On October 1, 1881, the *Norfolk Landmark* reported,

> *From all the indication, this line and combined rail line will have for one week at least a business altogether unprecedented in the South...it will be seen that the Chesapeake & Ohio will be a large contributor to be handsomely rewarded for its efforts in building the Yorktown Branch.*

Working day and night, on October 14, 1881, the first locomotive arrived by schooner at Newport News and was sent over road to Williamsburg. With a temporary track laid on Duke of Gloucester Street in Williamsburg, passengers could come in from there and Newport News. Transporting the military was primary to the celebration, and on October 17, a thirty-car train heavily loaded with passengers and military traveled to meet the readiness of the opening day celebration in Yorktown.

At the same time, the *Ariel* of the Virginia Steamboat Company left Norfolk and Portsmouth around six in the morning. There the gleeful passengers could connect to the new railroad in downtown Newport News on their way to Yorktown. The completion of all this modern transportation was reported to be the subject of many celebrations and speeches.

With transportation in the ready, the stage was set for a large crowd. Again fifty thousand participants jammed into Yorktown, with steamers *Northampton* and *Eliza Hancox* making alternate trips every ninety minutes between Norfolk and Newport News to connect to the new and exciting Chesapeake and Ohio Railroad.

Spectators arrived on the special spur from Lee Hall into Yorktown that was added from the Chesapeake and Ohio Railroad line to Newport News. The train ran up Goosley Road with preliminary plans to run beside the battlefield to

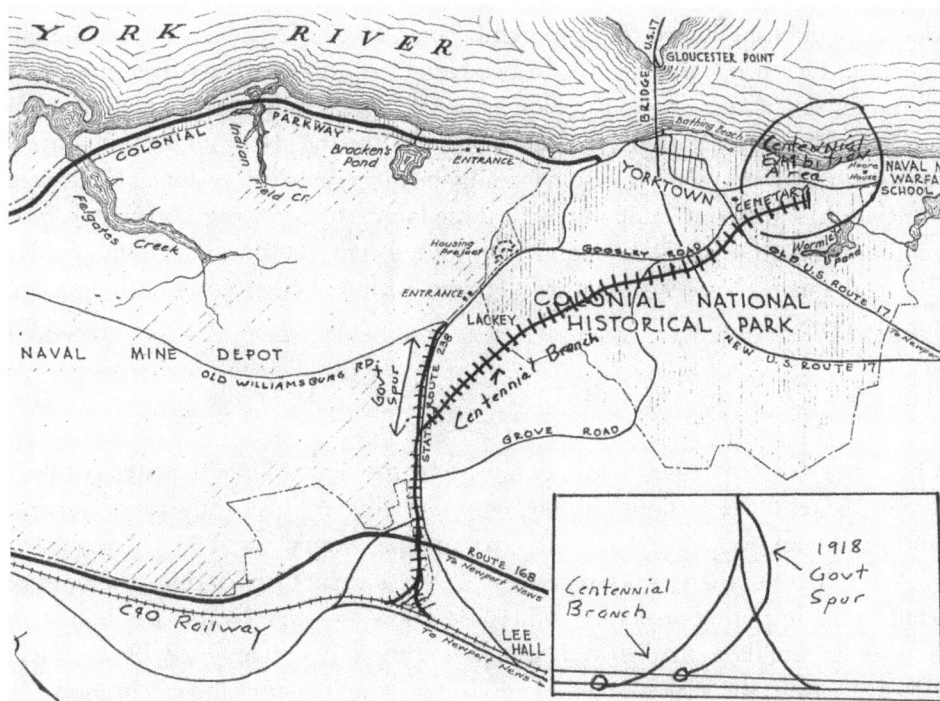

Map of the railroad spur to Yorktown. *Courtesy of the* C&O Historical Magazine, *August 1987.*

disembark their passengers at the Moore House. Failing that, the rail line "eased past the U.S. Soldiers Cemetery [located just off Hampton Road, known later, as Route 17], and ended its memorable trip about 1,000 feet past the first parallel, which was in the middle of the encampment area for the 1881 celebration. The Yorktown line ended there at a makeshift depot."

One of the first passengers from Newport News, Charles William Baines, a young boy at the time, remembered the first ride to the Centennial celebration. The C&O Railroad had made transportation possible in the fishing village of Newport News. Dressed in "somber Victorian attire," and invited by Collis P. Huntington, everyone, including the leading citizens, came in droves to the unsheltered switching track at the waterfront where Eighteenth Street intersects the north shore of the James River. With no building for a ticket lobby or waiting room, still the crowds gathered around the track for their first train ride to Yorktown. The train, a new dark green polished locomotive, delivered only days before by a four-masted schooner, was standing on the track that crisp fall day.

The train left downtown Newport News at somewhere between nine and ten in the morning as the formal ceremonies began at eleven. First-time riders were quoted in published stories later, remembering that "the locomotive began to puff, snort, and screech," and the ride to Lee Hall took thirty to thirty-five minutes.

Baines could remember the "long line of horse-drawn carts [and] wagons loaded with fine, fat York River oysters, brought into the celebration encampment area by local oystermen to assist in feeding the huge crowd of visitors." He added, "one could satisfy one's appetite with these large, super-flavored bivalves served on the half-shell, with all the fixings, for just ten cents per dozen. And hot coffee, like York farmers' wives know how to make, with real cream, right off the farm for five cents a cup."

Tuesday, October 18, 1881

On October 18, at 10:00 a.m., a concert by the Third United States Artillery Band played ten selections. Following, approximately twelve thousand foreign and American troops paraded with color and pageantry.

At 11:00 a.m., there was a reception for the governor of Virginia at Lafayette Hall. This imposing structure, otherwise known as the Grand Pavilion, was a wooden building that served as a convention hall. Designed by architect Albert L. West, the structure was demolished sometime after the celebration.

When the reception ended at noon, Grand Marshall Robert Enock Withers lead a procession to the monument site. In a show of power, the grand marshal marched with other Masons with their swords drawn. A prayer was read by the Reverend Robert Nelson, grandson of Governor Thomas Nelson, followed by

1881 medallion. *Courtesy of the Karwac Collection.*

"Centennial." *Courtesy of the Library of Virginia, Richmond, Virginia.*

a vibrant "Star-Spangled Banner," sung by three hundred voices accompanied by the prestigious United States Marine Band. Governor F.W.M. Holliday gave opening remarks followed by the "Marsellaise Hymn" and "Hail Columbia." The army, as well as the ship's guns anchored in the York River, fired loud salutes as the American flag was raised at the Victory Monument site. Along with the celebrations, a box of precious items were placed in the cornerstone and dedicated that day. The contents of the cornerstone capsule are listed in appendix A.

Harper's Magazine, in its post-celebration edition of October 29, 1881, commented:

> *On the land the transformation was as wonderful as on the water. The village had expanded into a city of shanties, tents, and booths, and its quaint brick courthouse had become a lodging house, as had most of its still quainter pre-Revolutionary building. Its streets, no longer grass-grown, were heavy with the continuous passage to and fro of a thousand teams, and thronged with a relentless multitude of sight seers, soldiers, vendors, gamblers, thieves, and itinerants of all kinds, whose shouts of laughter blended with strains of martial music and the thunder of heavy guns.*

In the raw photographs taken during the events, the visitors are standing in very close proximity to one another. Bearing up under the congestion, visitors heard hymns alternating with speeches that went on for some time. A concert by the First United States Artillery Band played another ten numbers. A Silver Cornet Band played ten numbers, creating a patriotic swell that nagged a teetotaler to the tavern. Peanuts, popcorn and pumpkin pie were available at the roadside, and bourbon sours, in honor of the French allies, were a good elixir.

That evening at 7:30, a show of fireworks from the boats in the river showed nineteen types of rockets and shells. At 8:30, a promenade concert and a hop with the Second United States Artillery Band were held at the reception hall.

Wednesday, October 19, 1881

The following morning of October 19, at 9:00 a.m., the red-coated United States Marine Band, lead by the twenty-seven-year old John Phillips Sousa, played nineteen numbers followed by an assembly at 11:00 a.m., called to order by John J. Johnson, chairman of the Centennial Commission. The United States Marine Band played an overture and the Reverend William L. Harris of New York led the prayer. A Centennial hymn was sung, and with all the anxiety

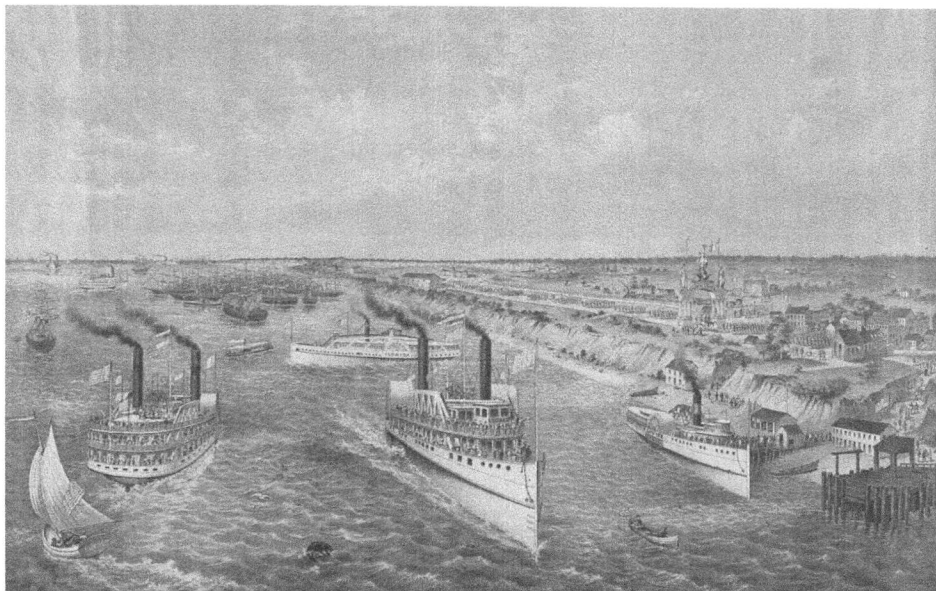

"Yorktown harbor and Centennial grounds." *Courtesy of the Mariners Museum, Newport News, Virginia.*

of the assassination of James Garfield in the air, a speech was heard by Chester A. Arthur.

Even though there was tremendous national unity, there were reports of great tension. It was not so long ago that the troops who now camped together had stood opposing each other in the Civil War. Having had two presidential assassinations in one generation, it was conceivable that Chester A. Arthur would be at risk. Yet appearing to be fearless, the president "bore up well."

James Garfield was on the minds and mourning bands on the sleeves of some attending officers. To some of the ex-Confederates present, the Yankee generals on the scene brought back unpleasant memories. William Tecumseh Sherman stood tall and erect in uniform. Once the scourge of Georgia, he was now the nation's top general. Also conspicuous were Philip Sheridan, Irvin McDowell, John Pope and others who had fought against the Confederacy between 1861 and 1865. The commission put General Winfield Scott Hancock in charge of the military units in town. Hancock had served in the Peninsula campaign of 1862 and at Gettysburg, then later lost to Garfield by only a narrow margin in his presidential race. Known for his even temper, the concern for any strife was eased.

Representatives of the French and German honorary guests made speeches saying that they were so grateful to be in attendance and did not "hesitate to brave the terrors of the ocean." Five verses were read of the "Centennial Ode," written by Paul H. Hayne. Robert C. Winthrop gave a Centennial oration, which he read from twenty pages.

A poem ten pages long of metrical address by Captain James Barron Hope was heard. The Thirteenth Regiment Band of National Guard of New York played an overture with the secretary of state, Honorable James G. Blaine making his speech. Ex-Senator Robert Winthrop of Boston spoke for nearly two hours, saying, "We are here to revive no animosities…rather to bury and drown them all."

At 4:00 p.m., a grand concert at the monument site provided ten numbers that were heard by Dodworth's Thirteenth Regiment Band. Separately, but at a similar time, the Legion Cornet Band in Dress Parade of Regiment Troops played in front of the Pavilion in honor of the guests.

Another pyrotechnic display was seen at 7:30 p.m., with the river twinkling in a sea of lights from the many hundreds of small boats anchored in the river. At 8:30 p.m., a concert by the Boston Cadet Band, J. Thomas Baldwin, conducted ten numbers played for listening enjoyment. The top hats could come off and the ladies could promenade their fashions for another reception and hop at Lafayette Hall.

Thursday, October 20, 1881

At 10:00 a.m., there was a grand military review as well as a naval review with fourteen ships in the river giving a sail drill exercise by unfurling, shortening and furling the sails of its ships. Because the president had to be back in Washington on October 21, the events of two days were combined. A river-facing grandstand allowed guests to view military drills performed in the river, followed by a band concert conducted, once again by bandmaster John Philip Sousa, who became famous for his military march compositions.

Virginia's Restoration

When the celebration was concluded, the C&O decided to abandon the rail service to Yorktown. After learning of the railroad's intention, Yorktown citizens were prepared to file a lawsuit to keep the tracks in place. When Huntington learned of the citizens' filing, he ordered all the tracks to be taken up, quietly, between Lee Hall and Yorktown. The materials were loaded on freight cars and hauled back to the main line before the local court could rule on the matter. The shock and disappointment was tremendous—the residents were let down with the loss of service and the disappearance of the tracks.

In the years preceding the Centennial celebration, the Yorktown-Williamsburg area had suffered some devastating losses. That year the College of William and Mary had been closed in 1881 and remained so until 1888. Many grand old homes were burned or pillaged to the extent of their loss. But for James City County, the county of Williamsburg, the greatest loss had been the destruction of their record books, which had been taken to Richmond for preservation but were lost in a fire that destroyed that city in 1865.

In trying to preserve the history of Yorktown, the Yorktown Centennial Association, which directed the celebration, tried to purchase the Moore House where the terms of the Revolutionary War surrender had been drawn. The Temple Farm five-hundred-acre site was to be donated to the Federal government for preservation as "Lafayette Park." The members tried to enlist private contributions, but the response was so poor that they were forced to sell the property to satisfy the creditors. Even with continued Federal, legislative and private interested parties, the Moore House continued into the late 1920s under private ownership.

With the purpose to acquire, preserve and restore historic grounds, buildings, monuments and tombs in the Commonwealth of Virginia, the Association for the Preservation of Virginia Antiquities was planned in 1888. A charter of incorporation was received by 1892, and by 1889, Mrs. Fitzhugh Lee, wife of the governor of Virginia, became president. Their first acquisition was the Powder Magazine in Williamsburg, with plans for the rescue of the Jamestown site from further shoreline erosion.

Virginia, finally left in peace times and not yielding to despair, was replenished anew by rebuilding the spirit that carried into the construction of a monument standing for the victory for which the town could be so proud. The work of erecting the granite Victory Monument took nearly two years—in 1884, it was finally completed.

The Centennial celebration awakened new life and brought new light to the spirit of unity. Robert C. Winthrop, disciple of Daniel Webster, speaking at the ceremonies said, "It is not by assassinating Emperors or Presidents that the welfare of mankind or the liberty of the people is promoted…Above all, the Union must be preserved."

THE SESQUICENTENNIAL
OF 1931

A Stellar Year

For so much of Yorktown, 1930 was a most pivotal year. The town had to be readied to accommodate the large numbers of people who would be attending the planned celebration. Yorktown was a struggling community without water or sewage facilities, electric lights, efficient roadways or mass transportation. There was one dilapidated pier from which the Chesapeake Steamship Company docked twice daily and the town was miles from the nearest railroad. Yet still, because the celebration was eminent, through contributions and cooperation of various civic, governmental and military groups, the work of installing all the roads and utilities was completed in that one stellar year.

Rich in heritage and history, the soil was forthcoming with relics of the past historic sieges, but some of the redoubts or places of surrender were taken away by wind and water erosion to the point of desolation leaving wood and gullies. *Putman's Monthly Magazine*, in July 1854, stated that the American breastworks were nearly obliterated but that there were still British entrenchments in perfect condition.

By 1924, the General Assembly of Virginia adopted a resolution to have five representatives from the House of Delegates and the Senate appointed to arrange the participation in this celebration.

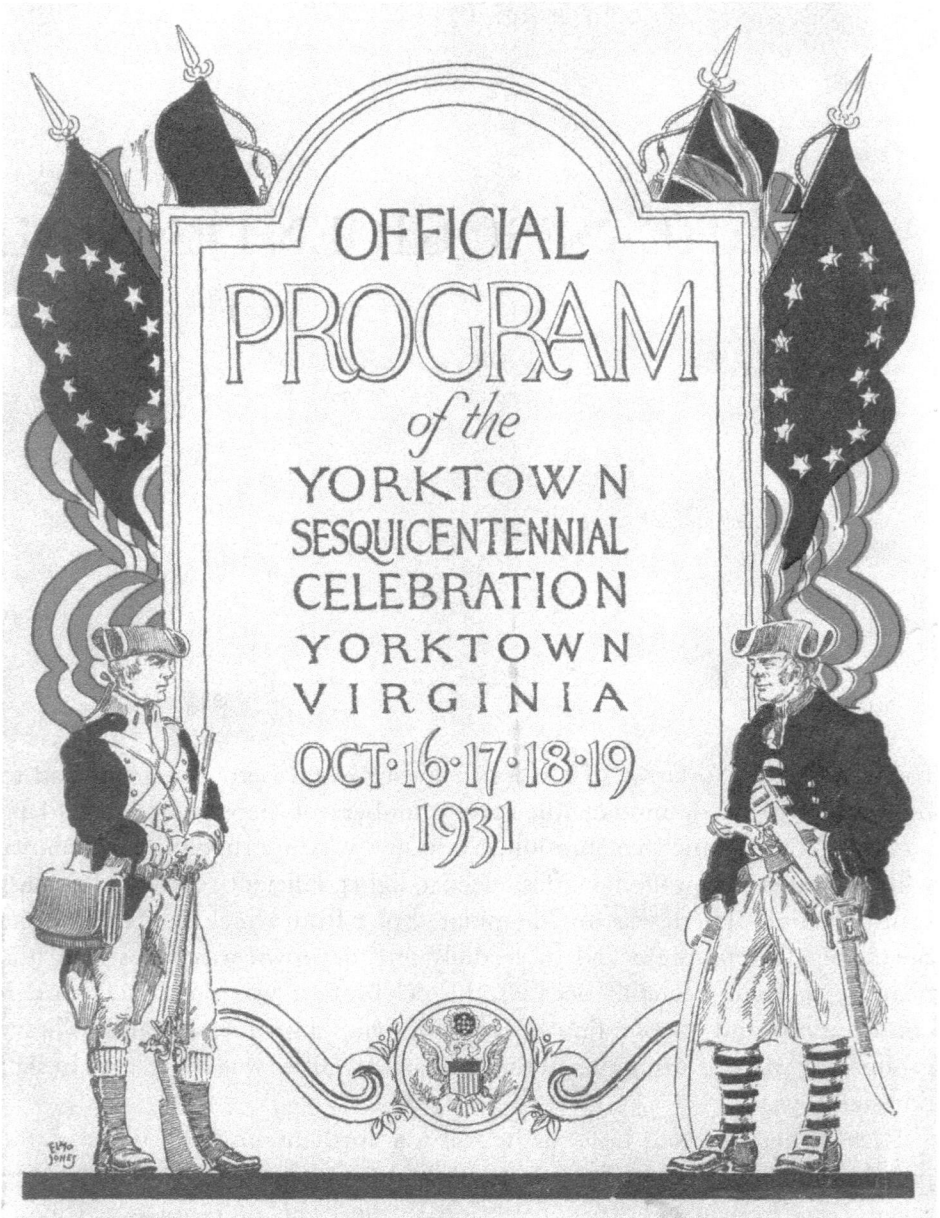

Cover of the 1931 sesquicentennial program. *Courtesy of the Manley Collection.*

By October 18, 1930, the United States Commission was in the making, with representatives meeting in Richmond to discuss and make promises of cooperation for the upcoming plans. On Monday, October 20, 1930, many of those same representatives met in Yorktown for the celebration of the 149th anniversary of the surrender hosted by the Comte de Grasse Chapter of the Daughters of the American Revolution.

Piped Water, Electricity, Telephone Service and Telegraph to Yorktown

The day after that 1930 celebration, all the representatives, which included the United States Commission, the Virginia Commission, the Army, Navy, the National Park Service, the Virginia Conservation, Development Commission and the Yorktown Association, started considering preparations for the celebration. S. Otis Bland, a member of the sesquicentennial committee wrote, "the magnitude of the difficulties immediately became obvious," but representatives of the National Park Service promised the United States Commission that if appropriations could be made for the establishment of the Colonial National Monument, a permanent installation of a water supply with a distributing system and sanitation facilities would be added in Yorktown.

In November of 1930, with the work of chief engineer Oliver G. Taylor and sanitary engineer Harry B. Hommon, along with plans of the army camp and the secretary of the Yorktown Association, estimates were put into place with Director Arthur E. Demaray of the Colonial National Park Service to secure appropriations for the Colonial National Monument and the Sesquicentennial Celebration.

The Virginia Electric & Power Company donated thousands of dollars for construction service for the increase of facilities in the streets at Yorktown. With the extension of the transmission lines between Yorktown and the celebration area, ample lighting was available for the tents, with flood lighting at the grandstands, both sides of all the arches, the colonial fair and all throughout the festival.

Yorktown also reaped the benefits of having the telephone system added to the utilities in town. The Chesapeake & Potomac Telephone Company of Virginia took on the project of installing telephone conveniences with a central office established at Yorktown during the celebration. Prior to the celebration preparations, the closest telegraph service was in Lee Hall. Now, along with the addition of the telephone system, the Postal Telegraph-Cable Company established temporary telegraph offices in Yorktown and the celebration area.

Left to right: Major Harold Kroner, executive of the United States Yorktown Commission; Representative S. Otis Bland, of Virginia, chairman of the United States Yorktown Commission; Dr. William A.R. Goodwin, chairman of the Yorktown Sesquicentennial Association and Brigadier-General Stanley D. Embick, commander of all military units. *Courtesy of the Haskett Collection.*

New Roads and Acquisitions

When the corporation first organized, it was understood that Dr. Julian A.C. Chandler, who was previously involved in the initial stages of the celebration, could not continue as president of the planning committee due to his responsibilities as president of the College of William and Mary. It was in October of 1930 that Dr. W.A.R. Goodwin was named president of the Yorktown Association that was one of the local planning committees for the celebration. Goodwin's strong association with Bruton Parish Episcopal Church and his close relationship with John D. Rockefeller Jr. made him a good leader for such a large undertaking in Yorktown. An early associate of Goodwin's summed up the "authentic hero and dreamer" by saying, "His eyes are deep set and overhung by bushy brows, the face is large and broad, and his whole makeup is stocky and strong. 'Very glad to know you, Mr. Houck,' he said, and I felt the pressure of his hand clasp for a full twenty minutes."

It was not going to be easy to draw the plans for the layout of the celebration. With the real estate of the entire battlefield still under ownership of a northeast development company and facing possible subdivision, and with the Moore House moved or torn down, the fate of the Yorktown land was unknown at the time.

Congress had begun a feasibility study in 1921 to establish a national military park at Yorktown. This was not the first attempt to establish a park; the planners of the 1881 Centennial had also proposed that funds be raised for the establishment of a park that would have included the battlefield and five hundred acres (including the Moore House). The Moore House acreage had already been purchased by private donations with the agreement that at the close of the 1881 celebration, the land would be donated to the United States government and be called Lafayette Park.

Early in 1924, the commission reported favorably and as a consequence, a bill was introduced in Congress to begin acquisitions of these sites. In 1926, John D. Rockefeller Jr. helped start the movement of preservation by the acquisition of the Moore House and a portion of the land believed to be part of the Surrender Field with the understanding that the federal government might acquire this property later in July of 1931. Eventually 1,961.78 acres would be acquired by the National Park Service, but for the time being, the property owners had to be considered in the preparations that lay ahead.

When legislation for the creation of the Colonial National Monument became law on July 3, 1930, Horace M. Albright was appointed director of the National Park Service. In a letter, Albright wrote, "I am so enthusiastic over this proposed Historic Park that I can hardly restrain my imagination. Unquestionable it will be the most famous park in the world almost immediately upon its establishment." And so it was that the National Park Service began their important work with the responsibility of the upcoming celebration. Acting as superintendent of the federal site was W.M. Robinson Jr.

In the beginning of the National Park Service's work at Yorktown, the Yorktown Hotel (Somerwell House), was acquisitioned and became the headquarters for the Colonial National Monument, later to be called Colonial National Historic Park. Alterations were completed and office furniture was purchased so the directors of the monument site could organize the permanent personnel for administrative and development purposes. The historical research, along with cooperating with the United States Commission for the Sesquicentennial Celebration, has become a priority.

By January 14, 1931, two hundred and fifty people had applied for work on the celebration, but a seemingly small force was hired. Fourteen miles of new roads were built, and many clay and secondary roads around the town were widened or resurfaced. Because the exact measurements of the "metes and bounds," were not yet decided, the park service only had description maps to determine the area that would be affected by the celebration. With added cooperation, the Virginia Highway Department planned to spend forty to fifty thousand dollars to build new roadways to help with the traffic flow and congestion. Ballard Street was extended with improvements to the Hampton Highway, and all the roads were subgraded in anticipation of the heavy traffic that was expected. By January 13, 1931, the construction offices were located in the Renforth Building on Monument Road (now called Zweibrucken), near the corner of Monument and Main Streets. The Yorktown Sesquicentennial Commission was also located there to coordinate projects. Colonel Harley B. Ferguson, previously of the Army, and Commander W.A. Pollard, formally of the Navy, both acting as engineers, began to make plans so the site could begin to be cleared. It was decided that both the parade grounds and the campsite would be down the old Hampton Highway, later called Cooke Road.

Washington Avenue, now known as Surrender Road, was built and acted as the central thoroughfare. Approaching from Yorktown on the left during the celebration, across from the grandstands, the plans allowed for fields of cotton, peanuts and tobacco, which were the crops that were most featured in the colonial period. Also located there were the tents for patriotic societies, bandstands and concession tents. Under large tents there were restaurants with carefully supervised food provided at reasonable prices, as well as lunch and soft drink stands.

Feeding the public was a chief consideration, but twenty-five hundred regular army troops also had to be fed. Procuring supplies so as to reduce the slow moving motor transportation congestion was a problem. Detailed deliveries were worked out so carefully that the trucks were off the roads before 8:00 a.m. Throughout the celebration, departure from the commissary at Fort Eustis permitted the actual unloading at the kitchen by dawn each day.

The setting of the tents for the public and the guests was a tactical feat in itself. The designated area was mapped and ten thousand pegs were driven, fixing the position of the tents. The speaker stand was in the center for specially invited guests. Behind the grandstands was the court of honor, designated by a series of arches and thirteen huge pylons to honor the original thirteen states. The tentage was acquired from the Army war reserve stock stored in the Philadelphia Quartermaster Depot and lent for the duration of the celebration.

The area selected for the celebration included an assembly field with plans for a Colonial Fair and Harvest Festival. Exhibition halls were inside tents and a separate Indian village was peopled by descendants of the Mattaponi and Pamunkey tribes of the colonial days. A large dance floor was set inside a tent

Tent city for soldiers at Yorktown. *Courtesy of the O'Hara Collection.*

and there were enclosures for the children with a Maypole dance and other amusements of "Punch and Judy" shows, marionettes, one-act plays, legerdemain (magic shows) and other amusements.

Exhibits of the old-time agricultural implements, old kitchen and house utensils and colonial costumes were on display. A section of the grounds was reserved for wild animals prevalent in colonial times. Deer, wild turkeys, bears, foxes, raccoons, opossums, wild duck, quail and grouse along with an exhibit of the Virginia Department of Agriculture were featured in that section.

Along with the assembly field, a performance area was created in a large cleared field with grandstands surrounding the area in a semi-circle. In the center of the pageant field was a special elevated stage. This modern stage was seven feet high and simple in design with steps and an electric elevator that could raise and lower for changes in the scenery and for the principal performers underneath the platform.

Seating the guests for the activities and entertainment meant building a large grandstand area. Large numbers had to be considered, so the grandstands were planned to seat 22,500, with the central stand of 7,000 that seated specially invited guests including distinguished Europeans, federal and state commissions

Publicity brochure of 1931. *Courtesy of the Karwac Collection.*

Grandstand crowds for Sesquicentennial, 1931. *Courtesy of the O'Hara Collection.*

and those of the Yorktown Sesquicentennial Association. In addition, there were 7,500 seats set aside for patriotic societies, state commissions and the public. An additional 5,000 seats were reserved for the use of Army, Navy, Marines and Coast Guard. Pictures of the time show a veritable sea of hats worn by ladies and men that were the fashion.

Assembling the huge grandstands was monumental and almost literally last minute—the heavy timber wasn't available until the day before the celebration. General Stanley D. Embick of Fort Monroe, had the daunting task of supervising preparations for the celebration. The military, being largely a part of the celebration, rushed to Embrick's side, along with other workers and labored long into the night. Even though there was work to be completed the morning of the first day, Oliver G. Taylor, engineer for the National Park Service engaged at Yorktown, assured everyone that the stands would be ready for the opening ceremonies.

It was good planning that regular military troops were quartered in the tent city. At this celebration actors and military soldiers garbed in colonial costume went through many rehearsals. People were converging on Yorktown to witness the colorful pomp and pageantry with thousands, upon thousands already there

Oct. 19, 1931
YORKTOWN SESQUICENTENNIAL
ASSOCIATION

AUTOMOBILE PARKING RECEIPT
Parking Fee 25c

Lot _____ J

No. _____ J14777

See Conditions on Other Side.

Parking pass. *Courtesy of the Karwac Collection.*

The United States
Yorktown Sesquicentennial Commission
requests the honor of your attendance
at the ceremonies in commemoration of the
One Hundred and Fiftieth Anniversary of the
Surrender of Lord Cornwallis
at Yorktown, Virginia
October sixteenth to nineteenth
Nineteen hundred and thirty-one

Admission to grand stand
by card only

Special invitation. *Courtesy of the Karwac Collection.*

in participation of the festivities. Long before nightfall the hotels on the peninsula were filled and private homes were already occupied.

Arrival of the French Delegation

The scene was an excited one as the French delegation arrived at Fortress Monroe. Everyone pictured wore the finest in fashion. General John J. Pershing, Governor John Pollard, Senator Claude A. Swanson, Senator Charles Crisp, Representative S. Otis Bland and other members of Congress were at the dock to meet the arriving party. Mrs. Woodrow Wilson, widow of the president, stood on a balcony overlooking the scene, as did several hundred people amid many military uniforms starched and pressed with plumes and military ribbons at the New Chamberlain Hotel on the waterfront in Hampton. Also in attendance were cabinet officials, high-ranking officers of every branch of the armed forces as well as most of the governors from the original thirteen colonies. The Lord Cornwallis, a lineal descendant of the famed British general, and his lady attended as well.

Three American cruisers were the first to welcome the French delegation with a roaring seventeen-gun salute at dawn the day before the celebration began. At 8:22 a.m. the French arrived at Hampton Roads and docked at approximately 11 a.m. The big guns bellowed their welcome from Fortress Monroe. After a short review of the troops, Marshal Philippe Pétain, the representative of France, was escorted to his quarters in the Chamberlain Hotel amid the United States Army Band playing military marches.

With so many speeches to be heard and re-enactments and pageants to be seen, an accounting of all the activities would be impossible to contain in one chapter. Therefore, a reporting of some of the events appears in the upcoming events.

Friday, October 16, Colonial Day

Along with all the heavy work the night before the opening day ceremonies, heavy rains came causing some water to pool in the lowest points of the pageant field. The water was quickly removed by pumps provided in advance for just such an emergency. The daunting rain laid the dust, so for the rest of the four days the sun shone brightly with cool clear weather making outdoor exercises comfortable.

Promptly at 9:00 a.m. on October 16, 1931, reveille was heard near the headquarters tent. The Army encampments area opened thirty minutes later with visitation until 11:30 that morning.

On this same day and throughout the celebration, with the exception of the last day, the fleets of ships anchored in the York River were open to visitors with launches running back and forth from the wharves. There were a total of forty-one ships in the river including the frigate *Constitution*, which received over sixteen thousand visitors. In the evening, all of the ships turned on their brightest lights and flooded the banks of the river with illumination that gave the spectators quite a show.

On the first day, two memorial dedications were offered. A plaque was given by the Sesquicentennial Committee at the Nelson House and a bronze tablet at the Customs House, gifted by Major William Besse of Torrington, Connecticut, and unveiled by Mrs. George D. Chenoweth.

There was controversy with the announcement of a plaque given on the property wall of the Nelson House honoring the British General Cornwallis. The controversy was concerning the political sentiment of the celebration organizers. There was talk that the focus of the surrender might be omitted from the program in deference to better world relations. Both Senator S. Otis Bland and W.A.R. Goodwin supported the idea because they wanted "to emphasize a triumph of ideals rather than to glorify a war victory or someone's surrender." The local press and foreign press were critical of such unnecessary sensitivity. In the final ceremony when the British flag was pulled aside to show the plaque, Major Rochambeau, adopted great-great-grandson of the French ally of Washington, spun about and came to a full salute.

GRAND STAND FOR ESPECIALLY INVITED GUESTS

The United States Yorktown Sesquicentennial Commission

ENTER AT GATE	YORKTOWN	SECTION
6	SESQUICENTENNIAL CELEBRATION YORKTOWN, VA.	H

SUNDAY, OCTOBER 18, 1931

GOOD entire day and evening   ADMIT ONE

Grandstand ticket. *Courtesy of the Karwac Collection.*

At noon the crowd at the grandstands was wowed when bugles blasted and the salute of seventeen guns heralded the arrival of Marshal Pétain. Huge crowds cheered as they recognized Pétain by his sky-blue uniform. General John J. Pershing accompanied Pétain in an official automobile and then entered under the Virginia arch. Standing atop the grandstand during remarks by the famous visitor were details of sailors from the French cruiser *Duquesne* that stood at attention with fixed bayonets.

Tilting Tournament

At 2:00 p.m., with the bright October sun brilliantly shining against intermittent puffy clouds, a tilting tournament (billed as one of the special events of the celebration) was staged at the pageant field. Thirty-seven knights costumed in knee breeches, brocaded coats and powdered wigs of the colonial period, astride sleek horses gallantly rode proud for their intended princesses. The men galloped down rows of steel rings with lances intended to tip the rings, as opposed to another rider. Only twenty-four remained after elimination, but three withdrew due to low score.

Applauding the difficult feats of the horsemen was a grandstand filled with ladies dressed in their colonial finery waving their lacy handkerchiefs. The intended prize for the ladies was to be named queen by the victorious rider for the planned dance that evening. At 7:00 p.m. the ladies were to march in a coronation parade that would throne the queen and name her maids of honor. Prizes were awarded for the best colonial attire and there was good-hearted but well-intended rivalry for the prize.

Lewis McMurran, a bright high school student of Newport News High School, prepared the pageantry of the tournament. McMurran would later be instrumental in many projects to beautify and celebrate Yorktown. Years later he was elected to the newly created Newport News-Warwick seat in the General Assembly of Virginia, and in 1947 he became the chairman of the bicentennial celebration of 1981.

Pageant of the Colonies

The pageant of the colonies depicted scenes of the history and characters of the thirteen colonies. All the actions on the field were repeated before the center, right and left grandstands. The audience only had to watch the station in front of its respective stand to see the entire action. Amplifiers located on the ground beneath the lower rows of seats carried the voices of the actors. The pageant closed with the participants dressed in the colored apparel such that when seen from the audience, the actors formed a living map of the nation when it was thirteen colonies.

Several of these pageants were performed on different days of the celebration. The themes were varied but related to the landing at Jamestown, the Yorktown campaign, and the surrender scene.

Saturday, October 17, Revolutionary Day

With the crowds of people arriving for the opening events of the second day, the Coast Guard band played a series of patriotic music, and a tablet was dedicated that still can be seen today on the front of the old Customs House. Addresses were given by Benjamin N. Johnson, president general of the National Society of the Sons of the American Revolution. In addition, the French Marquis de Chambrun and Marquis de Grasse made speeches with an acceptance speech by Mrs. George D. Chenoweth on behalf of the Comte de Grasse Chapter of the Daughters of the American Revolution of Virginia. Nearby on the sloping front lawn of the home of Eugene E. Slaight, Nicholas Martiau, an original patentee, was honored at that place which was thought to be the site of his home. Speeches were given by General John J. Pershing, General of the Armies, and Samuel Herrick, president general with the Reverend John Bear Stout, D.D. Today, that rough slate with a bronze plaque is still standing in the front yard of that house.

Along with many exquisite treasures and artifacts on display in various places at the old Customs House was a lock of Washington's hair and a piece of

1931 Washington head medallion souvenir. *Courtesy of the Karwac Collection.*

Washington souvenir pin. *Courtesy of the Karwac Collection.*

1931 souvenir pin. *Courtesy of the Karwac Collection.*

Washington's wedding vest. Also on display was a fish server, which was formerly the property of Governor Thomas Nelson Jr. There was continental currency as well as old congressional medals. Also among the treasures were publications: *History of the World,* by Sir Walter Raleigh printed in 1652 in London; a Bible printed in 1763 and a prayer book printed in 1761, formerly owned by Governor Thomas Nelson Jr. There were other publications dating from 1621 to 1752 and newspaper clippings of Lafayette's arrival in 1824.

With music by the Third Cavalry and Twelfth Coast Artillery Band, a pageant of the Yorktown Campaign by the military and the Navy was depicted at the pageant field, and later that evening the detachment of the Third Cavalry gave a lance drill, tandem, Cossack and sheik riding. A special drill was given by Battery A, Sixteenth Field Artillery as well as the Twelfth Coast Artillery with the air corps giving an exhibition of anti-aircraft firing.

This anti-aircraft firing was a spectacle that would not have taken place in any festival today due to safety factors. But on the nights of October 16, 17 and 19, five sixty-inch searchlights were placed at five locations for the demonstration. Two searchlights were on a road nearby and three on Surrender Field for the illumination of the targets. Two three-inch anti-aircraft guns were at Surrender Field each evening, and four machine guns were mounted in a parking lot near the camp hospital. The machine-gun fire was spent over the Newport News watershed property which adjoined the property.

Each evening a plane from Flight A, Seventeenth Observation Squadron, Langley Field, would act as a target flying up the York River at the altitude of six thousand feet. As the planes were picked up by the searchlights, the blank ammunition would fire in an attempt to illustrate how a plane could be shot down. In dramatic effect, the plane would go into a quick dive and the search lights were turned off with the pilot firing a bright flare to give the effect of a direct hit. Then with a sleeve target in tow, the aircraft was then re-illuminated and the machine guns would fire with intention of hitting the target in tow. After four times across the field the demonstration was complete. In the darkness with the glow of the flares and the movement of the light against the sky, the audience could hear a public announcer describing the event as it took place.

Sunday, October 18, Religion Day

It was exactly one hundred and fifty years ago on a Sunday (October 18, 1781) that the terms of capitulation were negotiated at the Moore House. It seemed appropriate that this day would be spent in religious services on the same day in 1931.

At 8:00 a.m. a Holy Communion at Grace Episcopal Church in Yorktown was given by the Right Reverend Dr. Arthur C. Thomson, bishop of southern

Virginia. Later, at 9:30 a.m., Catholic field Mass, with an interpretation in French, was given at the Pageant Field by the Reverend Richard Blackburn Washington, pastor of Sacred Heart Church, Hot Springs, Virginia, and great-grandnephew of General George Washington.

At 10:30 a.m. an assembled audience was called to order at the pageant field by the Honorable Hiram Bingham, senator of Connecticut, who introduced the Reverend Andrew J. Renforth, pastor of the Church of the Disciples of Christ, Yorktown, Virginia, to preside at the Union services. Music was provided by the United States Marine Band and a choir of fifty people. A resounding choice of music included "The Battle Hymn of the Republic," "Onward Christian Soldiers," "My Country 'Tis of Thee" and "America the Beautiful" among many others. The prayerful service contained responsive readings, an invocation by the Reverend John J. Scherer Jr., DD, of the Lutheran Synod of Virginia, and lessons from the Bible. The Right Reverend James E. Freeman, DD, bishop of Washington, read a sermon that was several pages long.

That afternoon at 4:15 p.m. a military religious service was attended by approximately ten thousand members of the Army, Navy, Marine corps, Coast Guard and National Guard. A processional march began the service with massed buglers. The United States Army Band played "America the Beautiful" as the prelude. Also, there was a series of invocations, scripture lessons, vocal solos and an address by the chief of chaplains, Colonel Julian E. Yates.

Although the religious ceremonies were the focus of that day, a pageant was performed that depicted the plan of the campaign in Yorktown. In a rousing scene set with the conferences and meetings between Washington and his generals, the depiction was intended to tell the story of the anniversary of the surrender on October 17, 1781.

From 7:00 p.m. to 8:30 p.m. a reunion was held on the pageant field for seventy-five people who had been in attendance of the 1881 celebration. Moments of reflection were special as John Phillips Sousa was in attendance of both these events. Sousa, who was now the lieutenant commander, had previously conducted the United States Marine Band on October 16 to play "The Royal Welsh Fusiliers" and "The Centennial March." That evening, however, the music was furnished by the United States Coast Guard Band for all that attended, including a special dignitary who had come from Sweden to attend this celebration.

Monday, October 19—Anniversary Day

President Herbert Hoover arrived October 19 and was met by salutes from all the naval and coast guard vessels that were present. His arrival on the pageant field

President Hoover arriving at the pageant field, 1931. *Courtesy of the National Park Service, Colonial National Historical Park at Yorktown Collection.*

Marching in the military review, October 19, 1931, military volunteers are costumed as Washington's continentals. *Courtesy of the O'Hara Collection.*

at 10:30 a.m. was honored by a twenty-one-gun salute as he passed under the Virginia arch. A troop of cavalry, with lances and guidons (flags), accompanied him to the speaker's stand where he was welcomed by thunderous applause.

The Reverend Dr. William A.R. Goodwin, rector of Bruton Parish Church and known as the father of the restoration of Colonial Williamsburg, opened with the invocation:

> *Lead us from this day, with finer patriotism and deeper consecration, into a richer future, and hasten the time when the love of power may find its fulfillment in the power of love which will abolish fear and hate and create among the nations enduring peace to the glory of Thy name, through Jesus Christ our Lord. Amen.*

The president gave a fairly lengthy speech and stated the purpose of the day was to "pay homage to a glorious event in our national history." At the conclusion of the address, the chairman of the commission awarded the president, Mrs. Hoover and Marshal Pétain gold badges which had also been presented to each of the especially invited guests.

Exercises were resumed on the pageant field by 1:45 p.m. with music by several bands and a pageant portraying the surrender of General Cornwallis. The scene was dramatically played out with "The World Turned Upside Down" playing softly along with the authentic portrayal of the surrender.

Following the pageant was the grand military and naval review. More than ten thousand soldiers and sailors marched before President Hoover and guests. Parading with the military units were military bands, including twelve service bands and marching units of visiting organizations. It gave the audience the opportunity to see all the units in their special formations, one after the other.

The exhibits and the Colonial Fair and the Harvest Festival continued until 10:00 p.m. But by the time the troops disbanded and departed the field, the tiny town of Yorktown was once again quiet and quaint. It had been awakened by the ceremonious activity with over 100,000 visitors to Yorktown over the four day celebration. But Yorktown was ready to return to the quiet afforded to a small town. Joseph S. Edgerton, staff correspondent to the *Washington Star* wrote:

> *With pageantry and military pomp and splendor on a scale seldom, if ever before, seen in a State which has known more battles and campaigns than any other in the Union, Yorktown, in the lengthening shadows of an October afternoon, yesterday completed the celebration of the One Hundred and Fiftieth Anniversary of the Surrender of the Army of Cornwallis and the realization of American Independence.*

JAMESTOWN'S 350TH ANNIVERSARY OF 1957

To begin to understand the impact of the size and scale of the large celebration that came to be known as the Bicentennial of 1981, it is best to understand the work of the celebration of 1957, Jamestown's 350th Anniversary. Many communities and a few in foreign countries participated in the 1957 celebration. As a result, vast improvements on the peninsula were needed to carry out that celebration.

The General Assembly of Virginia began the plans of the 1957 celebration of the Jamestown Festival in 1952. Delegate Lewis A. McMurran Jr. introduced a resolution that would provide for a preliminary commission to begin planning for the celebration. Construction of the Jamestown Festival Park was achieved through the cooperation of both state and federal agencies with specialists, many of whom worked without charge because of their interest in the project. Acting as the federal commission administrative director, Colonel H.K. Roberts, USAF, Ret., served as the contractor's representative for the festival mall buildings. The executive director of the Virginia 350th Anniversary Commission was Park Rouse. State Commission Director of Special Projects King Meehan filled a similar role for the fort area of the park.

In 1781, Yorktown was a well-populated port town of British America, but by 1952 when the planning began for the anniversary, it had one-fourth of the inhabitants. The construction had already begun some years before, but a long

Former Representative Louis J. Cramton presents to Superintendent Stanley Abbott the pen used to sign the 1930 law for federal protection of the area. *Courtesy of the Haskett Collection.*

envisioned highway that would connect Yorktown, Jamestown and Williamsburg was finally becoming a reality.

Much development on the peninsula had changed the environment of the park since its beginnings in the 1930s. A huge oil refinery was preparing to establish itself on the York River. The George P. Coleman Memorial Bridge, opened in 1952, replaced the ferries that had once crossed that same river. With the park yielding its holdings to Yorktown, York County schools, the Coleman Bridge development, as well as the naval installations for national defense purposes, the National Park Service needed greater development for public use.

An "improvised atmosphere" of a temporary information or Visitors' Center at Yorktown had been housed in the restored Swan Tavern, which had been reconstructed in 1934. In the rear was a ship exhibit with artifacts recovered from the York River by an underwater archeological project constructed between 1934 and 1935 by the National Park Service and the Mariners Museum at

Newport News. The exhibit was housed in a stable outside the Swan Tavern and the administrative offices were divided there and in other office spaces. It was the plan to construct new visitor centers at Jamestown and Yorktown with the completed parkway joining them.

Working together with Jamestown and the Association of the Preservation of Virginia Antiquities (APVA), the Park Service wanted to have visitation and preservation on Jamestown Island. A visitors' center was built to house exhibits, a film program and a collection of Jamestown artifacts that were uncovered by the park service during twenty years of archeological work on the island. In keeping with seventeenth-century history, a glass house factory for the recreation of glass crafts that were introduced to the American continent 350 years ago was also recreated near the 1608 foundations.

The Jamestown Festival Park would become a separate but new reality. As the Williamsburg center would provide a necessary visitors' center in that historic city, so would the festival center serve those coming to Jamestown. A welcome court with flagstaffs and an information center would greet the visitor with halberdiers from the James Fort that hoisted flags everyday at 10:00 a.m. This was the point where Vice President Nixon spoke on May 13, and Queen Elizabeth II responded to Governor Stanley's welcome on October 16, 1957.

So now there were three entities supporting Jamestown. The APVA, the National Park Service and the State of Virginia were all serving in the rather small acreage of Jamestown to have the largest celebration yet.

It is noteworthy that all such projects requiring time and careful management for the presentation of important history often had little preparation time because the requests had to be made with the state general assemblies for funding that same year. The state commission staff began its operation on July 9, 1954, and presented a completely formulated festival concept for funding in 1956, just nine months before April 1, 1957, when the festival facilities were opened.

The developments of the Festival Park, the James Fort, the reconstruction of Powhatan's Lodge, the Old and New World Pavilion and the building of three ships, *Susan Constant, Godspeed* and *Discovery*, along with other features of the park, would make an authentic statement to the visitors of Jamestown.

The Old World Pavilion was based on the heritage and ideals of the British and American people. This pavilion was built in three sections, to show the development of the British Commonwealth during the sixteenth and seventeenth centuries and building a free and peaceful world. The New World Pavilion was presented in two sections that provided a link between the original colonists in 1607 and their descendants.

The reconstruction of Powhatan's Lodge portrayed the important part that the Indians played in Jamestown's history. The lodge was thirty-six feet long and sixteen feet wide and was constructed in a framework of saplings that were bound together at the top with rawhide to create a series of arches. Over the framework, mats of cattail leaves were woven together with hemp thread. Inside the lodge were various objects portraying an Indian ceremonial lodge. Outside the lodge, visitors could view many objects such as a nearby log canoe, a field of Indian tobacco and a dance circle of seven poles. During the official festival, tribal members of the Rappahannock Powhatan Confederacy exhibited the customs and costumes based on careful research.

With research under the direction of Charles E. Hatch Jr., chief of research from the Colonial Historical Park, the data provided direction for the building of the James Fort. The fort was triangular with three bulwarks or walls of defense. Inside the fort the church building was the center of interest; the other buildings gave the visitors a new perspective on life in early America.

The building of the three ships became the symbol of the Jamestown Festival. The work was started in March and the vessels were christened on December 20, 1956—the 350th the anniversary of the first sailing. The replicas are authentic in tonnage, size and type. The merchant vessels were built of hand-hewn timbers and fitted with flaxen sails. From March 22 to the 25, the ships went to Washington, D.C., for a preview showing.

With the development of the Jamestown Festival of 1957, the idea emerged that visitors would start their tours in Jamestown, the site of important events from its founding in 1607 until it ceased to be Virginia's capital in 1699. The drive on the Colonial Parkway ten miles inland would go to Williamsburg, the official capital until 1780, at which time it was leading the country as the center of cultural and political events. The final phase of the tourists' visit would be another twelve-mile link to Yorktown, where American independence was achieved in 1781.

The first state commission became concerned with two problems for the celebration—transportation and housing. Because of the enormous projection of tourism to the area, a plan was set into motion that would be called Mission 66. With the expectation of eighty million visitors by 1966, roadways would have to be completed. Plans began immediately for roadway and bridge improvements. For housing, it was considered, but abandoned as impractical, to investigate the possibility of a floating "ship city" by using idle maritime fleets of ships on the James and the York Rivers.

Renovation and Innovations

Although the roadway that connected Yorktown to Williamsburg was begun in 1931, the project needed to be completed to Jamestown. The surface construction of the parkway was produced by brushing the surface cement and washing with acid to create the pebbly effect that was carried out the whole length of the roadway. Overlooks, parking areas and bridges over creeks were planned. Some seventeen thousand trees and shrubs were planted to create a finished landscape throughout the entire length. More than thirty interpretive markers distinguished by a blue-gray color with dark lettering, each bearing a seal characteristic of Yorktown, Williamsburg and Jamestown, were created by Prison Industries Division and the District of Columbia Department of Corrections, Lorton, Virginia. The last construction carried out in 1957 was the Ringfield Plantation picnic area, which was open to the public in the late summer of the anniversary year. With all completed, the Colonial Parkway was open from terminus to terminus (Jamestown–Yorktown) on April 27, 1957.

A principal concern at Yorktown was a battlefield tour road and an excavation that led to the discovery and reconstruction of Redoubt No. 10, previously swept away by erosion. This redoubt, or soldier-built fortification along the battlefield, was famous for being the place where four hundred Americans stormed the British, forcing the surrender. In this hallowed place the surrender was won with the articles of capitulation, later drafted at the Moore House, for the official surrender of October 19, 1781.

When Yorktown's Lady Liberty at Yorktown's Victory Monument was beheaded by a lightning strike in 1942, Oskar J.W. Hansen, of Charlottesville, Virginia, was commissioned to create a new statue. The graceful replacement lady was mounted on September 10, 1956. This time, a four-inch core was drilled from top to bottom to thread a steel cable that would serve as a lightning rod and support for the shaft.

1957 Visitors' Center at Yorktown with an observation platform on the roof. *Courtesy of the Haskett Collection.*

With the work completed, the monument was rededicated on October 19, 1957.

Plans for the visitors' centers were signed by Superintendent Stanley Abbott of the National Park Service in May 1955, at both Jamestown and Yorktown. With both buildings being designed as one-story buildings, the lowest bidder set the bid at $247,300 for the Jamestown center and $285,150 for Yorktown. Construction began in March of 1956 to house office, exhibit and storage space, as well as auditoriums that would seat two hundred people. Yorktown's center was completed in mid-February of 1957.

The installation of exhibits began in both centers, with the story of Yorktown showing an important town of the eighteenth century—a tobacco port—moving quickly to the convergence of the hostile armies upon the town with a large diorama showing the surrender at Yorktown. On a hatchway looking downward was the ship exhibit including a full-scale section of the British frigate *Charon*, scuttled in the York River.

The exhibit concluded on the first floor with Washington's sleeping and dining tents, acquired sometime between 1954 and 1955 for the sum of ten thousand dollars, of which half was donated and the other half appropriated by the federal commission. General Washington's tent had been kept and preserved by George Washington Parke Custis, the general's foster son and heir, since the Revolutionary War. Custis's descendants, the Lee family, had preserved the old tents but sold the outer cover of the dining tent to Pennsylvania's Valley Forge State Park. Fortunately, even the original pegs, poles and ropes were acquired with the purchase at Yorktown.

Arrival of British Royalty

Jamestown was host to the Queen of England and Prince Phillip on October 16, 1957. The royal couple flew into Patrick Henry Airport and were taken to Jamestown for various presentations of gifts along with some touring of

Williamsburg and Jamestown.

The commemoration of the siege and victory at Yorktown was held October 18–19 and called "the great event of the Festival year." The event was carried out by two commissions and eight organizations—the Comte de Grasse Chapter of the Daughters of the American Revolution, Society of the Cincinnati in the State of Virginia, Sons of the Revolution in the State of Virginia, Virginia Society of the Sons of the American Revolution, the American Friends of

Queen Elizabeth II and Prince Philip aboard one of the three ship replicas, 1957. *Courtesy of the Haskett Collection.*

1957 battlefield reenactment. *Courtesy of the Manley Collection.*

Lafayette, National Society of Children of the American Revolution, Trustees of the Town of York, the Colonial National Historical Park and Alexander Hamilton's Bicentennial Commission. These organizations were instrumental in coordinating the pageantry and assisting in bringing descendants of the French leaders of the battle of Yorktown.

On October 11–21, 1957, the second army stationed at Fort Monroe, along with the Armored Cavalry Regiment of Fort Knox, Kentucky, provided the necessary Army personnel and equipment to place an equipped camp for four to five hundred men on the Yorktown battlefield. Units of the twenty-five Centennial Legions from other states, along with six fife and drum corps from Connecticut, participated in ceremonies. Representatives of the original thirteen colonies were in attendance with eleven of the thirteen governors present.

The two-day program was celebrated with two anchored Navy vessels holding open house. In town, fife and drum corps maneuvers could be seen during the parade. A concert was planned for that evening by the United States Army Band with a fireworks display, but inclement weather caused most of the first day's events to be canceled.

On the second day of the program, 2,500 people attended the rededication of the Victory Monument ceremony at Yorktown. Later that day there was a reenactment and other pageantry was viewed by the visitors that numbered about 25,000 in attendance on the battlefield.

With the year's end of 1957, the festival of the 350th celebration of Jamestown lasted eight months. With tremendous increases in visitation to the Jamestown-Williamsburg-Yorktown area, the Colonial National Historical Park estimated 2,158,107 visitors to the parks combined.

THE BICENTENNIAL
OF 1981

Celebration 1981

On the first day of the celebration, the weather was sunny and the air was crisp. Flags lined the streets of the town and the battlefield, snapping smartly with an autumn breeze. On the last day, though the weather began with mild conditions, by the afternoon a severe storm was moving toward Yorktown from the Williamsburg area.

Just a few months after President Ronald Reagan was shot in an attempted assassination, he was scheduled to attend the 1981 celebration in Yorktown. The president's address was the highlight event of the celebration, and as he delivered it to tens of thousands of visitors and VIPs, officials watched the stormy forecast and it became obvious that an evacuation was going to take too long to be effective. With most of the visitors having arrived by bus or a shuttle system, it was impossible to shelter everyone. The temperatures dropped and the winds picked up, but by the end of the day it got no worse and the storm never materialized.

The 1981 celebration was named the "Heritage Festival" honoring direct descendants of the key participants in the famous Battle of Yorktown. In attendance were Richard de Grasse, fifth-generation of French Admiral de Grasse; the Marquis de Lafayette; the Count de Rochambeau; President Ronald Reagan and French President Francois Mitterrand. "Our family has lived with

America's Victory
Celebration
at
Yorktown, Virginia
October 16-19, 1981

Official Commemorative Program
for the
200th Anniversary of the
Battle of Yorktown
1781-1981

Program of 1981 Bicentennial. *Courtesy of the Manley Collection.*

this inspiring legacy for a long time," said de Grasse. "And I'm very excited about going to Yorktown to participate in that heritage."

This celebration had been very difficult to plan because it was the largest with the most participants, and also because a directive of the White House caused an impact in 1974 that carried a ripple effect for years to come. James Haskett, retired chief historian remembered, "There was immense pressure from the White House to have everything in all the Revolutionary parks completed and up by January 1, 1976. It took several years before [the park personnel] were able to clear up all the problems this haste had generated."

And so it was that there were two bicentennials, the first being the national celebration, which in fact was more demanding than the latter because the activities were all over the country. Preparations for this celebration coincided with need to innovate at Yorktown for its own Bicentennial.

The Colonial Park Service Renovations

It had been twenty-four years since the visitors' centers were built at both Jamestown and Yorktown, consequently, simultaneously, the visitor centers had to be doubled in size, including the exhibitory and audiovisual facilities. The Nelson, Smith and Ballard Houses had to be restored. The Nelson House itself needed a complete renovation. But along with this renovation there were stage props and costumes added for actors that were hired for interpretation.

A new system of transportation needed to be in place for the battlefield area—the battlefield tour roads had to be updated, rerouted, and paved. In addition, an updated area had to be developed for Surrender Field.

A more modern maintenance area for the park service was relocated and built and a ranger station was developed on the Blow Estate (the newly acquired Nelson House).

The Somerwell House had to be upgraded and a new security and fire alarm system had to be installed to accommodate safety concerns and regulations. More research was conducted on the allies at Yorktown, the British defenses of Yorktown, Main Street, the waterfront, the Nelson House, the Smith House, the Ballard House and the Pate (Cole-Diggs) House, and archeology was expanded at the Poor Potters site, the Grand French Battery, center of the second siegeline and the Glasshouse at Jamestown. And finally, the installation of a bridge over Tobacco Road began that would connect the visitor center to Main Street.

With all the work that seemed insurmountable, there were meetings all over the country with other parks that were to be involved in the upcoming national celebration. The ever-growing number of visitors expected led to the installation of FEMA trailers, three at Yorktown and three at Jamestown, necessary installments for information desks, exhibits and films in each. Estimates by New York wire services stated that six hundred thousand people had visited Jamestown in 1973. The triangle of Jamestown, Williamsburg and Yorktown was about to be engulfed by visitors with the coming of the national 1976 celebration.

A large sum of money was designated to National Park Service for all the projects, but with the help of so few experienced staff members at the service centers, regional and Washington offices, retired senior historian James Haskett began to think that things were becoming "an incredible mess." At the time it was said that the only thing that was not under construction was the Jamestown Glasshouse, but in 1974, it burned down. In a matter of days the Glasshouse staff got a temporary operation up and running with the park engineer creating the Glasshouse design that was rebuilt on budget and ahead of schedule. This was not to be said of most of the other projects.

During the summer of 1976, there were over one hundred employees supervised by the acting historian James Haskett, including acting troops at the Nelson House, glassblowers at the Glasshouse in Jamestown and bus drivers for the transportation system, with a number of living history roles at both Jamestown and Yorktown. When the pressure of the 1976 celebration had passed, the task of preparing for 1981 began.

Planning the 1981 Celebration

There were major logistical problems for the committees to identify and solve. A temporary thirty-thousand-seat stadium had to be put in place, a temporary amphitheater had to be built and staffed, and a plan was needed for the development of a colonial fair. There had to be development on the waterfront including dredging the river, building boat landings and designing, building and funding a memorial plaza. Parking lots had to be constructed as well as a transportation system. In addition to everything that needed to be planned, expected visiting dignitaries and guests needed "requisite housing," which was a challenge, since Yorktown had few hotels in town. Lastly, the National Park Service wanted to help facilitate the manning, funding and support of the local Yorktown Bicentennial Committees.

Acting assistant chief historian, Diane G. Stallings, wrote in a memorandum of the Bicentennial in review, "My personal view remains that our division managed to overcome some very frustrating situations and handle massive amounts of visitors with tact, common sense, and shear grit." With the aid of festival display boards, numerous people were directed to daily events during the four-day festival. Because of the congestion at the five points area (the convergence of Ballard Street, Zweibrucken Street, Colonial Parkway and the entrance to the

Crowds in the grandstands, 1981. *Courtesy of the Margie Cox Collection.*

Visitors' Center), it became obvious that the park service personnel were performing protection duties, especially for crowd control.

The Visitors' Center saw over fifteen thousand people a day; with the need for more restroom and Port-a-John facilities, it even became necessary for administrative staff to tackle the problems of cleaning bathrooms due to overuse.

Phone and radio communication became confusing due to circuit overload, unnecessary duplicates of transportation for park personnel, and long hours of answering numerous phone calls about military, VIPs and congressional staff were handled by staff volunteering after hours.

In 1980, the board of supervisors for the County of York consisted of Chairman H. Tabb Smith, Vice Chairman Rogers A. Smith, E.S. Bingley Jr., Shirley F. Cooper and Benjamin M. Rush Jr. With funding for the Virginia Bicentennial Committee and separate funds established for the National Park Service to complete their tasks, the county needed funding from the state. In a letter dated January 5, 1981, the board asked Governor John N. Dalton for special funding of an estimated $200,000 as a one-time appropriation for "cleaning-up, fixing-up and sprucing-up Yorktown for which no funds are forthcoming except for local tax dollars."

The Yorktown Victory Center as it appeared in the late 1970s. *Courtesy of the Jamestown-Yorktown Foundation, Yorktown, Virginia.*

Victory Center

In April 1976, the Commonwealth of Virginia opened the Yorktown Victory Center as one of three Bicentennial centers operated by the Virginia Independence Bicentennial Commission. Twenty-one acres were donated for the site by local residents Nick and Mary Mathews. Delegate Lewis McMurran Jr., chairman of the commission, was on hand to assist Governor Miles Godwin's wife cut the blue ribbon at the entrance, flanked by authentically uniformed flag bearers of Revolutionary militia, surrounded by dignitaries from Britain, France and the United States.

British Minister to the United States John O.W. Moreton brought greetings from Queen Elizabeth II and spoke of his supersonic trip on the Concorde with the message that the United States and Britain, "once locked in the agony of war, are now firmly bound together by the bonds of alliance." Both France and Britain furnished the Yorktown Victory Center with treasures on loan that were representative of the Revolutionary era.

For the cultured attendees, the Victory Center displayed paintings from Paris, London and New York. Historical items like Lafayette's sword, Washington's diary and the surrender documents were available in a two-hundred-item exhibit. In 1982, after the Bicentennial of the American victory at Yorktown, operation

The ribbon cutting at the Victory Center. *Courtesy of the Jamestown-Yorktown Foundation, Yorktown, Virginia.*
Shown with Governor Mills E. Godwin, Jr. (far right) at the original dedication of the Victory Center in 1976 are (l-r) Lewis A. McMurran, Jr., chairman of the Virginia Independence Bicentennial Commission, John Warner, administrator of the American Revolution Bicentennial Administration, John O.W. Moreton, British minister to the United States, Jacques Kosciusko-Morizet, French ambassador to the United States, Mary Mathews, Mrs. Godwin and Nick Mathews. The Mathews donated the land on which the Victory Center stands.

of the Victory Center transferred to the Jamestown-Yorktown Foundation, which also operates Jamestown Settlement.

It was not just the museums or new indoor centers that benefited from the interest of the great artists; at Surrender Field, sculptor Felix de Weldon donated his time and $230,000 to complete his monument to Washington, Lafayette, Rochambeau and their horses. A plaster cast was made first, then set with a bronze paint and finished with a greenish patina to look like an authentic bronze monument. The monument measured forty-two

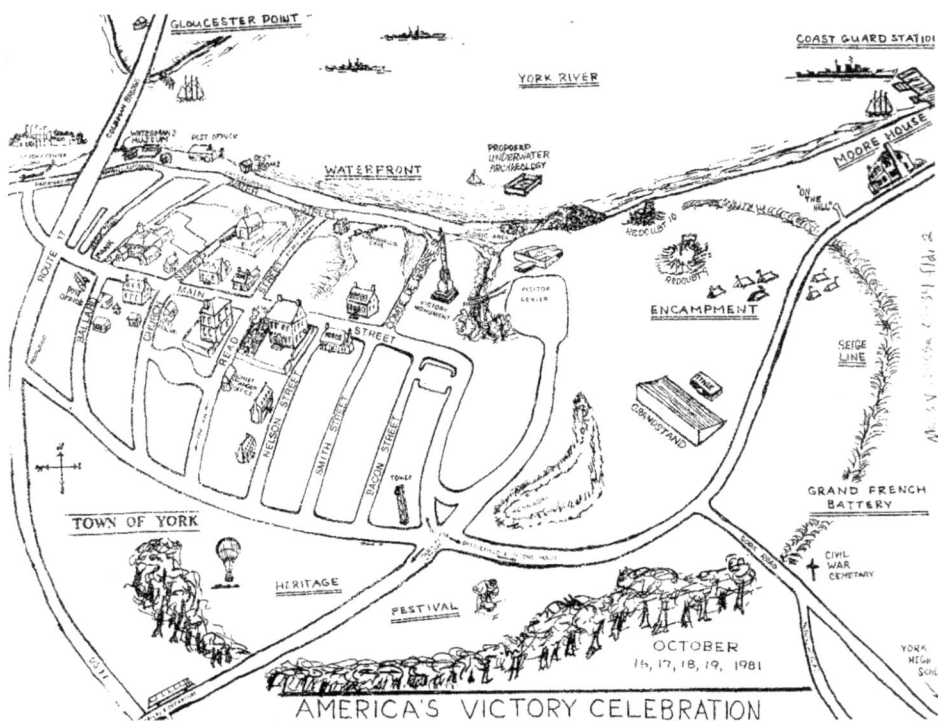

America's celebration, 1981. *Courtesy of the Manley Collection.*

feet long and twenty-six feet high. A portrait of the generals in motion on horseback in relief against a large rectangular shape, the monument stood at an angle on the edge of Surrender Field where the generals may have passed on their way to the final ceremony two hundred years ago. Following the bicentennial celebration, the monument was dismantled and relocated.

Celebration Organization

Similar to the celebration of 1931, the theme titles for each day were called Festival Day, October 16; Military Day, October 17; Patriot's Day, October 18; and Victory Day, October 19. The events of the celebration were spread between Gloucester Point, the York River, the waterfront, the Yorktown Victory Center, the encampments on the battlefield, the Heritage Festival (sixteen acres with ten theme areas of special entertainment), the Moore House and the Coast Guard station. In town there were ongoing events at the Yorktown Historic

Festival tent interior. *Courtesy of the Spivak Collection.*

Jousting tournament. *Courtesy of the Spivak Collection.*

area, the National Park Service Visitor Center and the Grand French Battery. Numerous displays were available to the public including exhibits, open house tours, museums, tours with interpretive programs, video tapes and both modern and eighteenth-century military displays.

The local people who lived in Yorktown were invited to participate. Many civic organizations assisted by giving tours and historical lectures on the colonial homes in the festival tent. Numerous people spent countless hours on the preparations long before the public ever came to visit. Others stood watch at various points on the celebration grounds to help with crowd control. The streets were closed off to outside traffic and sealed for security purposes making trips home at night almost impossible. Some locals who participated in the events remember sleeping on cots at the Baptist Church along with some of the other volunteers.

Within the Heritage Festival area a "theme center" featured "Yorktown Under Siege" with twelve mounted murals and photographs of private homes and public structures present in Yorktown during the Revolutionary War. Hostesses in period costumes interpreted the murals to visitors.

In the same area there was an "Ethnic and American Lifestyle Showcase" with two stage areas that featured traditional American performances in bluegrass, jazz, clogging and square dancing.

The Norfolk Tricentennial Exhibit celebrated Norfolk's 300th anniversary with exhibits displaying the town through the centuries.

The American Farm and Home Exposition was housed under two tents with craftsmen, artisans, potters, woodcarvers, instrument makers, quilters, cooks, blacksmiths, spinners and weavers displaying their talents. An agricultural exhibit showing what farm life was like in colonial times was pure family entertainment with pens of livestock that were indigenous to the colonial days.

A game and wildlife exhibit featured Virginia wildlife. There was also a large tank of live fish and marine life, wildflowers, food and old farm and forestry tools. A replica of an old trapper's cabin with peanuts and oyster shell handouts for the visitors was a true Tidewater festival happening.

Following the tradition of the 1931 festival, a colonial jousting tournament took place with forty knights from Virginia, Maryland and West Virginia. They rode their mounts over an eighty-yard course in eight seconds or less in an attempt to capture progressively smaller rings on the tips of their lances. Cash prizes and trophies were awarded to the winners.

For four hours each day under a separate tent, visitors could participate in a genuine auction of antiques, gifts and souvenirs. An Indian village within the Heritage Festival area featured three native Virginia Indian longhouses. The members of the Mattaponi Indian Tribe dressed in full regalia and displayed artifacts and beadwork along with displays and demonstrations. A special area for education and orientation information on all aspects of the festival was set to headquarter in the Heritage Festival tent.

The "Spirit of America" balloon, brought down from Philadelphia's 1976 celebration, flew boldly. This eight-story-high balloon was an unusual exhibit painted with scenes of the American Revolution.

The Events of the Celebration

On the first day of the festivities, a parade from the Victory Center to the battlefield started at 8:30 a.m. and was scheduled to pass the stadium/battlefield at 11:30. An assemblage of all the military units from every branch of service participated in the parade and the demonstrations in town. The parade also featured fifes-drum corps, floats and included Mattatuck Indians.

With all of the Revolutionary reenactment units included, more troops were in Yorktown than had been seen since 1781. There was local participation by school marching bands and open cars and floats from many civic organizations. Opening ceremonies included an address by Governor John N. Dalton and the undersecretary of the United States Department of the Interior, Donald P.

Virginia Military Institute Regimental Band. *Courtesy of the Spivak Collection.*

Hodel. Flag presentations and a bicentennial poem were heard in the ceremonies that started at noon.

At the end of the parade a special ceremony dedicated Zweibrucken Road (formally Monument Road) thus intertwining Yorktown as a sister city to Germany. The martial music began the swells of patriotism. Yorktown had many musical concerts throughout the celebration with the French Marine Corps Band, Turkey Run Orchestra, Second Marine Aircraft Wing Band, Merrimac Chorus, United States Coast Guard Band, Chesapeake Bay Bearcats, USCG Dixie Band, York High School Band, United States Atlantic Fleet Band, German Army Band, the Bicentennial Orchestra and the Bicentennial Chorus. In addition to the band concerts performed in different places in and around the celebration area, seventy-three entertainers were listed in the official commemorative program.

Throughout the four days, there were wreaths or presentations of busts, plaques, memorabilia and statue dedications. The dedications were held at the French Trench, the Victory Center, Grace Church, Moore House, Surrender Field, Redoubt Nine at the battlefield, Yorktown Victory Monument and the York County Court House. In some cases, formal ceremonies were conducted to honor various people or organizations. A time capsule was buried the last day at a ceremony at 3:30 p.m. and the contents (treasure of that time) were sealed in a twenty-by-twenty-by-twenty airtight, waterproof, capsule to be opened in 2031 (see appendix B).

Naval water demonstration. *Courtesy of the Spivak Collection.*

At the waterfront there were mock sea battles, water demonstrations, sailboat races, a navy motor whaleboat regatta, thirty-minute river cruises, sailing ships and vessels such as the *MEKA II, Dove* and the *Pride of Baltimore*. Jacques Cousteau's famed *Calypso* was on display at Gloucester Point, and the five anchored Navy warships had open houses throughout the day with launches available to the ships.

Across the river at Gloucester Point a seafood festival began on Sunday, October 18, along with an address by United States Congressman Paul S. Trible Jr. with French and United States military bands. With all the Chesapeake Bay's fare with cultural events and interdenominational religious services on the Yorktown battlefield, the mood was reverent, yet gala. Later that day there were fireworks lighting up the festivities on the York River.

Regiments depicted French, British and American officers and foot soldiers along with their camp followers. They did not laze about day-to-day, but acted as they would have by following the original military manuals. The four thousand reenactors were impressive and carried the flavor, sights, smells and sounds of the festival. Garbed in eyeglasses of proper shape and handmade shoes, every detail of their appearance was authentic—even their clay pipes were only lit with flint and steel. These men and women make this a year-round hobby and are dedicated to the lives of the Revolutionary soldiers. For five days the troops camped in tents that were of proper military dimensions (eight-by-fourteen-by-ten-feet). They also had large amounts of black powder for their muskets and cannons, which caused some concern at the beginning of the celebration. In a prelude to the four-day event, Rhode Island troops marched from their home state recreating the march of Rochambeau and Washington to Yorktown, fighting mock battles along the way.

As the centerpiece of the final day, there was a reenactment of the Battle of Yorktown. Dignitaries and the general public stood along the battlefield as the volunteers from twenty-three states fought a mock battle that had been planned as one of the most important events. The public reveled in the mock attacks on the British redoubts, demonstrations of colonial battlefield surgery, and finally the white handkerchief of surrender waved by the British.

Following the tradition of Chester A. Arthur in 1881, and Herbert Hoover in 1931, the appearance by President Ronald Reagan was a point of excitement, but extraordinary planning had to be put into place to secure his safety. After the speeches from the French president, French Francois Mitterrand and other national and foreign leaders, a grand military review of more than five thousand modern and Revolutionary War troops paraded past the presidential reviewing stand from 11:00 a.m to 1:30 p.m.

Each of the speeches had a decided focus on the longevity of the Franco-American friendship with toasts and good cheer. Mitterrand and his wife, Danielle,

Tall ships in the York River. *Courtesy of the Spivak Collection.*

Tents of the reenactors at the 1981 Bicentennial. *Courtesy of the Spivak Collection.*

Reenactors British Light Infantry. *Courtesy of the Spivak Collection.*

British grenadier reenactors engaged in a mock battle. *Courtesy of the Spivak Collection.*

Reenactors costumed as Washington's continentals in military review. *Courtesy of the Spivak Collection.*

were hosts at a Sunday lunch aboard the moored French frigate *De Grasse*. The presidents enjoyed dining on lobster and lamb. Later that day, the presidents, their wives and ninety-two other guests, amid fife-drum fanfare, attended a black-tie dinner at the Royal Governors Palace in Williamsburg.

At two o'clock that afternoon a special surrender ceremony was held at the stadium. The surrender ceremony that included three thousand Revolutionary War troops from twenty-three states and Canada recreated the historic surrender of Lord Cornwallis's forces to the combined American and French armies. Troops from America, Britain, France, Germany and Ireland were depicted as Governor John N. Dalton and other dignitaries were in attendance.

As with any large-scale event it takes much less time to disassemble an event than it does to put it together. For Yorktown, the rapid retreat of all the historical merrymakers was similar to a romantic night at its end. With 184,000 visitors in attendance it had been the largest and most successful of all the celebrations of the past. The events and their participants, sorry to end the festivities, were so thoroughly exhausted that many retreated to their private homes with close friends and strong libation.

A speech from President Ronald Reagan, October 19, 1981. *Courtesy of the Spivak Collection.*

The presidential reviewing stand. *Courtesy of the Spivak Collection.*

An eerie prediction appears in the vintage pages of the "Yorktown Book," which refers to the 1931 Sesquicentennial Celebration. Douglas Southall Freeman wrote a two-page piece opposite a portrait of George Washington that states:

What will be the significance of Yorktown to those who turn the pages of this little book in 1981 to see how their grandfathers observed the Sesquicentennial? The answer to that question lies with the prophet, not the historian; but if liberty lives, whatever its form it will be linked with Yorktown.

APPENDIX A
CONTENTS OF THE VICTORY
MONUMENT CORNERSTONE

After four years the Victory Monument was completed. When the cornerstone was finally laid with great ceremony, an interesting and priceless collection of items was placed inside.

- The Holy Bible
- 1783 United States copper coin
- A copper coin of Washington and Independence, 1783
- 1783 colonial coin
- United States silver coin of 1776
- Copper coin of 1787
- One-fourth franc
- Three metal medals
- 1859 one cent Canadian coin
- 1874 French coin
- October 1862 one hundred dollar treasury note
- One-hundred-dollar Confederate interest-bearing note
- One-hundred-dollar Confederate treasury note
- Copy of program issued at the celebration at Yorktown
- Photo of Confederate flags
- Yorktown Centennial medal

• Diagram of the cornerstone as furnished for the execution
• 1881 memorial of the schedule of arrival and departure of the mails
• October 1881 copy of the *Real Estate Journal*
• 1879 published copy of the *Travels of the Ego and Alter*
• Copy of the *Methods of Language*
• Teachings and a copy of the Yorktown Centennial volume
• 1781 copy of the Yorktown campaign and surrender of Cornwallis
• 1881 copy of the *Warrock-Richardson Almanac*
• Copy of the Charter of Yorktown Centennial Association
• 1824 bylaws of the South Carolina Commentary #1
• Joppa Lodge bylaws
• Copy of the sketch of the Solomon Lodge #1 and bylaws
• Bylaws of Winterpock Lodge #94
• Copy of a postal card calling a meeting to consider the centennial
• A leaf from the Bible on which George Washington was made a Mason
• Roll and members of 1881
• List of names of Yorktown Centennial Chorus membership ticket and song sheet
• Amity Lodge list of officers and members of 1881
• Masonic apron
• Copy of the "Washington and Lee"
• Copy of the proceedings of 1880 Grand Commandery of Knights of Templar
• Copy of official commissions and dispensations from Grand Chapter of Virginia
• Unabridged copy of *Webster's Dictionary*
• Full set of Lodge jewels of silver.

APPENDIX B
CONTENTS OF THE
1981 TIME CAPSULE

- Message from President Ronald Reagan
- Proclamation of President Ronald Reagan
- Proclamation of the United States Congress
- Message, John W. Warner, United States senator, Virginia
- Message, Harry F. Byrd, United States senator, Virginia
- Message, Paul Trible, United States congressman, Virginia
- Message, John N. Dalton, governor of Virginia
- Message, Virginia General Assembly
- Messages, York County Administrator
- Message and scroll, York County employees
- Resolution, Yorktown trustees
- Message, York County School Board
- Message and photograph, York County Bicentennial Committee
- Message, York County Planning Ordinance
- Message, York Exchange Club
- USGS topographic maps, York County (water/sewer/highways)
- Map of the state of Virginia
- Map of Virginia Peninsula
- Fiscal year 1982 budget, York County
- Fiscal year 1982 pamphlet, "Programs and People"
- Photograph, York County Board of Supervisors and Administrators

• York County seal
• Chart, York County political organizations
• Chart, York County administrative organizations and functions
• Resolution R78-256 (Sister City—Zweibrucken)
• Program for visit of Zweibrucken delegation
• Resolution P.81- 334 (Appoints Nelson & Marge Harris as "Keepers of the York County guestbook")
• Book, *Reflections of the Past*, by M.I. Bryant Jr.
• Bicentennial medallions, 1979, 1980 and 1981
• Coin, United States Prosf Sat, 1981
• Guestbook, 1931 returnee and theme center visitors
• Phonograph record, "Yorktown Salute," United States Army Band and Chorus
• History, Royal Deux-Ponts (Zweibrucken) Regiment
• History of Virginia boundaries
• Materials, Gloucester County
• Materials, National Park Service
• Brochure, "Yorktown Shipwreck Archeological Project"
• White House briefing book (Yorktown Bicentennial Committee)
• Bicentennial Calendar of Events
• Bicentennial *Citizens News*, (York County Information Office)
• Bicentennial program booklet
• Yorktown brochure
• Bicentennial program brochure
• Yorktown Victory Center brochure
• Virginia bicentennial guide
• Map essay, "The Surrender of Yorktown"
• Special editions, local newspapers
• Program, bicentennial victory bill
• Brochure, "The Ride of Jack Jouett"
• Pamphlet, "A Chronology of Yorktown" (Public affairs United States Army)
• Program, 1931 Sesquicentennial returns to 1881 celebration
• Program, the time capsule
• Program, lights of freedom
• Program, reception of the Zweibrucken
• Material from the Yorktown Bicentennial Committee
• Book of art, essays and poems by Virginia students
• Poem, "Ode to Yorktown," by W.O. Mahone, Harrisonburg, Virginia
• Message, Langley Research Center, NSAA

CONTENTS OF THE 1981 TIME CAPSULE

- Map, Colonial National History Park
- Excerpt, *The London Gazette*, September 12–16, 1695
- Letter from Lord Cornwallis, October 28, 1781
- Peninsula transportation report, 1981
- Peninsula economic base analysis
- Peninsula economic develop guide
- Letter, mayor of Berea, Kentucky

BIBLIOGRAPHY

"America's Victory Celebration at Yorktown." (official program, Virginia Independence Bicentennial Corporation, 1981).

Andersen, Kurt. "A Last Bicentennial Bash." *TIME*, November 2, 1981.

Bland, Otis. *The Yorktown Sesquicentennial*. Washington, D.C.: United States Government Printing Office, 1932.

Brandon, Edgar Ewing. "A Contemporary Account of the 'Triumphal Tour' of General Lafayette." (1824).

Brown, Alexander, C. "Lafayette's Triumphal Return to Yorktown, 1824." *Daily Press* (Newport News, Virginia), 22 February 1981.

Chesapeake and Ohio Historical Society, Inc. *Historical Magazine* 13, no.10: (October 1981).

Chesapeake and Ohio Historical Society, Inc. *Historical Magazine* 19, no.8: (August 1987).

Click, Carolyn. "4-day extravaganza includes President." *Public Observer* (Fall 1981).

Complete History of Marquis De Lafayette. S. Andrus & Son, 1846.

Corbett, Marjorie. "Yorktown Bicentennial." *National Parks* (September/October 1981).

"Descendants Participating." *The Advantage.* (Yorktown, Virginia), October 7, 1981.

Dill, A.T. *The 350th Anniversary of Jamestown 1607–1957.* Washington, D.C.: United States Government Printing Office, 1958.

Dunford, J. Vann. "Celebrations, Centennial and the Monument at Yorktown." *Daily Press* (Newport News, Virginia), October 17, 1954.

Friddell, Gary. "Miracle of Yorktown." Bicentennial Corporation, October 1981.

Gabriele, Virginia. "184,000 Flock Here for the BiCentennial Spectacular." *Yorktown Crier*, October 22, 1981.

Graves, Robert A. "Victory Monument." *Daily Press*, March 23, 1963.

Hall, Phyllis, A. "Yorktown Revisited." *Virginia Cavalcade* 31: (1981).

Hammes, Doris, P. "Had It Not Been For Lafayette." *Daily Press*, October 17, 1971.

Haskett, James. E-mail message to author, December 24, 2004.

Hatch, Charles Jr. "125th Lafayette's Anniversary To Be Heralded at Yorktown." *Daily Press* (Newport News, Virginia), October 16, 1948.

Idzerda, Stanley, J. *Hero of Two Worlds.* New York: Queen Museum, 1989.

Kinnier, Katherine. "Planned Communities Date to Colonial Period." *Daily Press* (Newport News, Virginia), November 8, 1973.

Klamkin, Marian. *The Return of Lafayette.* New York: Charles Scribner's Sons, 1975.

Knight, Don. "Forgotten Hero of '81 Honored by Two Nations." *Daily Press* (Newport News, Virginia), October 17, 1954.

"Lafayette's Lionized On Visit to U.S. He Helped Establish," *Daily Press*, October 13, 1940.

Levasseur, A. *Lafayette in America, Journal of a Voyage*. Philadelphia: Carey and Lea, 1829.

Lindgren, James, M. *Preserving the Old Dominion*. Charlottesville: University Press of Virginia, 1993.

Lyon, Ed. "Yorktown: The Town That Twice Lost Out on Permanent C&O Operations." *Chesapeake and Ohio Historical Magazine* 13, no.10: (August 1987).

Marth, Del. "A Bicentennial Finale." *Nations Business* (September 1981).

"Monumental Work Marked Centennial." *Virginia Gazette* (Williamsburg, Virginia), September 2, 1981.

National Park Service. Colonial National Historical Park. Archives. Yorktown Collection.

Reid, H. "Peninsula First Passenger Train Leaves for Yorktown, October 19, 1881." *Daily Press* (Newport News, Virginia), October 16, 1955.

"Report of the Virginia 350th Anniversary Commission," Commonwealth of Virginia, Division of Purchase and Printing, Richmond, Virginia, 1958.

Rouse, Parke Jr. "World Turned Upside Down 198 Years Ago at Yorktown." *Daily Press*, October 14, 1979.

Travis, Edward, G. "Richmonder Wins Tournament at Sesqui." *Daily Press*, October 17, 1931.

Tucker, George H. "Norfolk and the Revolutionary Centennial." Chap. 60 in *Norfolk Highlights 1584 - 1881*. W. S. Dawson Company, 1971.

"Vast Crowd Sees Sesqui Pageants." *Daily Press*, October 17, 1931.

Vivian, William. "The C&O Peninsula Extension," *Chesapeake and Ohio Historical Newsletter* 13, no. 10: (October 1981).

"Workman Begin to Clear Sesqui Area at Yorktown." *Daily Press*, January 14, 1931.

Yetter, George Humphrey. *Williamsburg Before and After: The Rebirth of Virginia's Colonial Capital*. Williamsburg: The Colonial Williamsburg Foundation, 2001.

Yorktown Book, The. Richmond: Yorktown Sesquicentennial Association, 1932.

"Yorktown Observes Its Bicentennial." *TIME* (October 1981).

"Yorktown Sesquicentennial Celebration Yorktown Virginia 1931 Yorktown Sesquicentennial Association." (official program, Lewis Printing Co., Inc, Richmond, Virginia).

"Yorktown Sesquicentennial Opens." *Daily Press*, October 16, 1981.

"Yorktown Victory Centennial, 1881." *Daily Press*, May 11, 1980.

ABOUT THE AUTHOR

K athleen Manley is a lifelong resident of Yorktown and a descendent of one of the generals in the Revolutionary War, Benjamin Lincoln. English, history, arts and the love of Yorktown are prominent interests. This is her second book on the history of Yorktown.

www.ingramcontent.com/pod-product-compliance
Lightning Source LLC
Chambersburg PA
CBHW070057100426
42740CB00013B/2853